How to Succeed in Law School

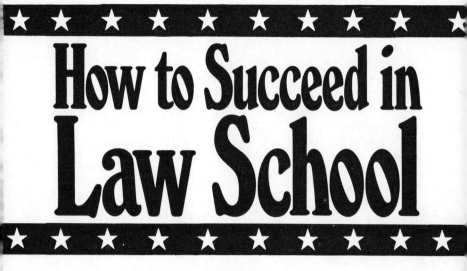

Brian Siegel

The author is associated
with the law firm of
Buchalter, Nemer, Fields & Savitch,
Los Angeles, California.

Barron's Educational Series, Inc., Woodbury, New York

All inquiries should be addressed to:
Barron's Educational Series, Inc.
113 Crossways Park Drive
Woodbury, New York 11797

Library of Congress Catalog Card No. 75-17848

Paper Edition
International Standard Book No. 0-8120-0609-7

Library of Congress Cataloging in Publication Data
Siegel, Brian.
    How to succeed in law school.
    1. Law students—United States—Handbooks, manu-
als, etc. I. Title.
KF283.S55   340'.07'1173   75-17848
ISBN 0-8120-0609-7

PRINTED IN THE UNITED STATES OF AMERICA

Dedication
To Marlene, the apple of my eye

Acknowledgments

The author would like to acknowledge the comments and helpful suggestions received from the following members of the California Bar: Stephen Chrystie, Benjamin E. King and Howard Coleman. Mr. Siegel is also grateful for the cooperation of Curtis J. Berger, Vivian O. Berger, Alfred Hill, Arthur W. Murphy, Albert J. Rosenthal, and Herbert Wechsler of the Columbia University School of Law; Dorathy W. Nelson and Albert Brecht of the University of Southern California Law Center; and the Foundation Press, Gilbert Law Summaries, West Publishing Company, and the American Law Institute.

Contents

Introduction

Almost all students entering law school are aware that a good legal education requires long hours of intensive work. Unfortunately, there is no necessary correlation between time expended and grades achieved. During my freshman year at Columbia Law School I studied approximately ten hours per day (exclusive of classes) and briefed virtually every opinion in my casebooks. In addition, I attended every lecture and took about three and one-half pages of notes per classroom hour. Finally, I constructed fifty to sixty page summaries (or *syntheses*) for each course. Despite the foregoing elaborate preparations, I instinctively realized that I was lost as I read the hypothetical questions which comprised the greater part of each final. The result of my concentrated efforts was a grade-point average slightly in excess of a B, which placed me somewhere between the top forty to thirty-three percent of my class.

The primary reason for this disparity between effort and achievement was my inability to effectively organize and apply the large volume of information I had amassed to the complex, issue-packed hypothetical problems which appeared on each final. Unhappily, it was not until I actually took the exams that I realized that there was a vast difference between reading and summarizing (or *briefing*) legal opinions which focused upon a clear-cut legal controversy, and, analyzing a paragraph-long description of unbelievable events from which the issues contained in an entire course were to be extracted and discussed.

A positive aspect did, however, emerge from my freshman year. One of my professors mentioned on the last day of his course that the only means by which one could hope to spot the numerous issues contained in a law school hypothetical within the allotted time was by utilizing a type of *checklist* composed of the important topics and doctrines in each course. These topics and doctrines are the sources of the issues which are embodied in the exam questions. I visited this instructor after finals and described the difficulty I had been experiencing. He admitted that he had not excelled in law school until he had learned to organize his work effectively. He then showed me the outline of the answer to the previous year's final in his course. I was surprised to see that it was only slightly longer than two typewritten pages, yet it covered about sixty percent of the issues encountered during the semester.

I began to realize that I had been guilty of two major study errors which many freshman law students undoubtedly commit. First, I had been attempting to apply the memorization-type approach which had been successful on the undergraduate level to the more analytically oriented law school exams. In college I had been able to remember finite masses of information and simply plug this data into the appropriate question with successful results: I had graduated Magna Cum Laude and had been elected to Phi Beta Kappa at Syracuse University. Law school exams, however, are designed to measure the test-taker's ability to isolate and discuss the particular legal issues which are embedded in each hypothetical problem. Second, I had failed to place my primary study emphasis on *understanding* the unique legal principles embodied in each opinion and their interrelationship. It is only after a student truly comprehends a proposition of law that he or she will be capable of recognizing and discussing it when it appears in an alien factual setting. Conversations with my classmates who had excelled academically confirmed these conclusions.

After my freshman year I began to develop a study procedure which emphasized the skills described above. As my learning techniques became more refined, my grade-point average increased correspondingly. Significantly, the methodology which I evolved was applicable to all of my courses. In my fifth semester, although I was enrolled in what were reputed to be several of the more difficult courses, I received three *Excellents* (the word equivalent of an A) and a *Very Good* (a B+). I was subsequently designated a Harlan Fiske Stone Scholar for academic achievement. I also received letters of commendation from my Evidence and Commercial Law professors for conspicuously well written exams.

The objective of the foregoing narration was not to impress the reader with the author's academic prowess; rather, it was intended to illustrate three important premises:

(1) Contrary to what is probably the general rule at the undergraduate level, there is no necessary correlation between time expended in study and the grades achieved in law school. Attempts to memorize, rather than understand, course materials will *not* succeed.

(2) A student may not realize he or she has been studying ineffectively until finals, when it is too late.

(3) If we assume that most students entering any particular law school class possess approximately equal intelligence and motivation, the common denominator which will characterize those who excel from the others will be the former group's grasp of legal principles and the unique nature of law school exams.

Unfortunately, most law schools provide little, if any, individual instruction or supervision after the initial semester has begun.

Ideally, a student should read the entire book before classes commence and then refer to the pertinent sections as the topics which are described are actually experienced. While it is difficult to impart a study procedure relating to a field which is probably new to the reader, increased understanding of the concepts which will be discussed should occur as the reader becomes more familiar with the basic materials upon which they are grounded. The first-year materials (primarily excerpts from commonly used Torts and Contracts casebooks) which are contained in the body of this book should assist the reader's assimilation of the study techniques which follow. Although this book was written primarily with the freshman law student in mind, the concepts discussed on the following pages should also prove quite helpful to students of any year and even those studying for the Bar.

One caveat is in order. The methodology propounded in the following pages does *not* represent a means of short-circuiting the many hours of study which are inherent in a good legal education. This work will merely provide the serious law student with a sense of direction which should enhance his chances of obtaining an academic yield roughly equivalent to the efforts expended. It is somewhat inequitable that some students achieve superior grades simply because they develop the knack for law school study and exam-taking prior to others. The prime objective of this work is to give all freshmen these insights, which in turn should result in grades becoming an exclusive function of hard work.

The Brief

The Casebook Method of Instruction

A fundamental assumption made in this work is that the *casebook method* of teaching is employed at the institution which the reader will be attending. Virtually all accredited law schools utilize this means of instruction. Each student is usually requested to purchase a casebook and supplemental materials (containing the most recent cases and legislation) for each course. The casebooks, thick one-volume works, have in almost all instances been authored by experts (usually law professors) in that area of the law. Most of the assigned materials will be contained in the casebooks, which can be perused in any legal book store. Thus, the casebook is the typical law school text.

Casebooks were undoubtedly so named because they are composed primarily of actual appellate opinions (or cases). An appellate court is one which reviews the decisions of the courts below it (usually the trial court). Many of these opinions will have been edited to omit those portions which are extraneous to an understanding of the legal principles which each case embodies. Sometimes these opinions are followed by abbreviated decisions which run only a few lines. The purpose of the abbreviated decisions is usually to expand or focus upon a specific aspect of the prior, lengthier decision. The opinions contained in the casebook are often followed by commentary which may (1) describe other examples of the proposition of law which the main case illustrates, and/or (2) raise questions concerning the applicability of the opinion to slightly different factual circumstances.

The Conventional Brief

A typical assignment in law school will be to *brief* the opinions contained in the next twenty pages of the casebook. A brief, theoretically, is a summary of the essential points of a decision. A dissertation on the manner in which a case is briefed is usually one of the first topics explained to incoming law students. The traditional brief dissects an opinion into five separate parts—the *Facts* or circumstances involved, its *Procedural* posture, the *Issue* or legal controversy which is the subject of the appeal, the *Holding* or the proposition of law which the case represents, and the *Rationale* or the reason why the court reached the result that it did.

The Facts are simply a statement of the circumstances which underlie the controversy. Obviously, the *plaintiff* (the party bringing the legal action) has concluded that he has suffered a legal wrong at the hands of the *defendant* (the party being sued) or a lawsuit would not have occurred. The acts or omissions the defendant committed and the consequences which resulted therefrom is the type of information collected under the heading of Facts. Although the relevant facts are ordinarily alluded to at the inception of a case, it is not unusual to discover them scattered throughout the opinion. An example of the Facts of a case might be something like the following: "Mr. A told B that if B would climb a particular flagpole, A would give B $5.00. B climbed the flagpole but A refused to pay him. B sues A for $5.00." An opinion must be read carefully to determine which facts were crucial to the court's decision.

The portion of the brief devoted to Procedure usually describes who was successful at the earlier stages of the litigation, what (if any) interim relief was granted by the lower court, and who appealed the earlier decision to the appellate court. Of course, the defeated party is usually the one which takes an appeal. Sometimes, however, the victorious party is not granted all of the relief requested, and appeals from that portion of the decision only. In a typical brief under the heading of Procedure, one might expect to find a statement such as: "Plaintiff won in trial court, defendant obtained a stay from the judgment pending its appeal, the appellate court rejected defendant's appeal, and defendant now appeals to the Supreme Court of the state." In short, this aspect of a brief sets forth the procedural history of the controversy. This information is almost invariably contained in the initial portion of the opinion.

The Issue is the legal controversy which the appellate court is being requested to determine. At the trial level there are often issues of both law and fact. However, appellate decisions, the type which are contained in the casebooks, are almost always concerned with questions of law. A typical statement of the Issue might ask: "Where A climbs a flagpole because B promised him $5.00, did B receive adequate consideration (a Contracts' topic) for him to be liable to A?" The findings of fact made by the lower court will ordinarily not be disturbed unless they are "clearly erroneous." Where the Issue is whether the lower court's ruling is justified by the facts, it would probably be framed as follows: "Where a father permitted his three-year-old son to play among other children with a golf club despite repeated warnings that the child was swinging it wildly, and the infant subsequently struck another child causing substantial facial injury, did the lower court erroneously conclude that the father had not been negligent under the circumstances?" Thus, two types of issues are (1) was the trial court's understanding of the law pertaining to the issue before it correct, and (2) assuming the correct principles or standards were applied, do the particular circumstances which were present require a different outcome?

A third type of issue which first-year law students will usually encounter only infrequently pertains to statutory construction. All jurisprudence is based upon either the common law or legislative enactments. The term *common law* refers generally to the body of law which developed from judicial (i.e. court) precedent spanning hundreds of years. In contrast, statutory law is the result of action by the legislature. Criminal Law and that portion of the Contracts' course which pertains to the Uniform Commercial Code are examples of the latter which are usually found in first-year subjects. Where the interpretation of a statute is at issue, it is important for the student to focus upon the precise word or words which are the subject controversy. An example of the phrasing of a statutory issue would be: "Were the goods delivered within a 'reasonable time' within the meaning of Section 2309 of the Uniform Commercial Code?"

The Rationale of a case describes the reason why the court decided the issue in favor of one party rather than the other. It is the element that usually comprises the major portion of an opinion. There are numerous grounds upon which a court can base its ruling. Every argumentative tactic ever devised has probably supported legal decisions at one time or another. The most important consideration is usually *stare decisis* (i.e. precedent). Reduced to its simplest form, this means that where an appellate court in the state has previously decided an issue in a particular way, lower courts and other appellate courts of equivalent rank are obliged to render a similar result. Where there is no precedent on a particular issue, courts may turn to decisions rendered in neighboring jurisdictions for guidance in handing down its ruling.

Where there are no appellate cases on point, a court will often examine the overriding policy behind the common law rule or statute which is most nearly applicable. For example, let us assume that there is a statute which prohibits anyone from charging an interest rate in excess of ten percent because any higher percentage would work an undue economic burden on the inhabitants of that state. A, despite having knowledge of this provision, charges B twenty percent for a loan of $100.00. When B fails to pay A at the end of the year, A sues B for $120.00. B not only alleges usury as a defense to the excessive interest, but also claims that he should not have to pay back any portion of the loan. The court might accept B's contention on the grounds that such a result would greatly discourage unlawful lending, and thereby promote the purpose which the statute was designed to achieve.

The argumentative technique of analogy comes into play when there has been a ruling on a similar proposition of law or set of circumstances. Thus, in a state where there are judicially created rules that (1) the seller has a "reasonable time" to deliver goods where no date is mentioned, and (2) the buyer has a "reasonable time" to reject goods which do not conform to contract specifications; a court could conclude that where a prior decision has construed "reasonable time" in the former instance to mean at least fifteen days, a similar interpretation should be accorded the latter.

Another means of persuading someone to accept a particular viewpoint, and therefore a ground for deciding a case, is by *a fortiori* logic. An example of this type of reasoning is the following: If A is taller than B, and B is taller than C, then A must be taller than C. Translated into a legal context, if one is liable for injuries caused to another from inadvertent, but negligent conduct, then *a fortiori,* one should be liable for damages which are the result of deliberate action.

Courts will also often justify their decisions by pointing out the consequences which would result from a contrary ruling. One of the principles of Torts law is that one is generally under no duty to come to the rescue of another. Thus, if Mr. A (a six-footer in perfect physical condition) sees a six-month-old baby drowning in two feet of water near him, Mr. A can simply ignore the infant with legal impunity even though the child could have been saved with only a minimal effort. While this probably seems unjust to the reader, the consequences of a different ruling might be even less desirable. If one is under a legal duty to come to another's rescue, where would this obligation stop? Would the reader want to be under a legal duty to attempt to save a drowning person, even though people in such a predicament frequently panic and pull their rescuer down with them? If you were to see A threatening B with a knife, would you expect to be liable to B if you failed to jump between them? The problem of drawing lines may be so difficult to resolve that a rule which in some instances may work a hardship upon innocent parties may nevertheless be the most feasible outcome.

Finally, courts will sometimes cite Restatements and treatises as authority for their decision. These works will be described more completely later. It will suffice to say for now that they pertain to specific areas of the law and have been written by experts in that field.

To summarize, in addition to precedent, any and all debating or editorial techniques for persuading people to agree with a particular viewpoint are embraced by courts to justify their ultimate decisions. When discussing an issue on an exam, a student is expected to make every possible argument which each side to the controversy would set forth to persuade the court to rule in its favor.

The last subheading of the classic brief is the Holding. This element is the most difficult to formulate. Opinions are placed in a casebook to illustrate the legal principles which comprise that particular field of the law. These principles should be reflected in the holdings. The holding will usually answer the question posed by the issue, but in somewhat broader terms. For example, where the issue was, "does one have a legal duty to attempt to rescue a drowning child?" the holding would be worded as follows: "One is under no legal duty to come to the rescue of another (even where it can be accomplished without danger to himself)."

Sometimes the holding of an opinion will simply be a standard or test, as opposed to a forthright principle of law. For example, it is often stated that one of the basic elements in a defamation action which the plaintiff must prove is that the defendant's statements and/or actions "impugned" the former's character. Thus, the holding of the case in which this criterion was found would be, "Defendant must impugn plaintiff's character to give rise to a defamation action." Such criteria must be applied to the

given facts of a test hypothetical, and are therefore fertile
sources of issues on an exam.

The Capsule Brief

First-year law students are invariably admonished that
reading and briefing each of the opinions contained in the
casebook is essential to academic success. While this is probably true in most instances, it is respectfully submitted
that the conventional method of briefing requires a student
to transcribe and focus upon much information which is
irrelevant for test purposes. The classic brief was probably
designed for the courtroom rather than law school, and
therefore it is of limited effectiveness in the latter context.

First of all, the unique *facts* of every case which a student has been read during the semester could not possibly
be repeated on a final. Even short-answer multiple choice
questions which sometimes comprise a small portion of a
final are rarely identical to a particular opinion. The hypotheticals appearing on law school exams test a student's
ability to spot many issues, and will probably bear little re-
semblance to the circumstances described in the individual
decisions contained in the casebook which focus upon a
single issue. The facts of a particular opinion are important
only insofar as they affect or shape the holding, and as such
would be incorporated directly into it. Obviously, law students could not be expected to commit to memory the
factual circumstances of the hundreds of opinions read
throughout the semester.

Similarly, it matters not one iota whether it was the
plaintiff or defendant who was successful at the earlier

stage of litigation, what the appellate procedure is called, or if a stay of the judgment has been obtained or not. With the exception of a course like Civil Procedure where the holdings are by definition principles of that body of law, the *procedural* segment of the conventional brief is unnecessary. Next, although you must understand the *issue* to accurately formulate the holding, it is not necessary to set forth the issue as a separate entity since it will be subsumed within the holding. As noted earlier, the issue is the legal question which is ultimately answered in somewhat broader terms by the holding.

The *holding*, or principle of law which the opinion was placed in the textbook to illustrate, is by far the most important aspect of any decision for exam purposes. *You do not know a particular case, regardless of how many times it has been read, until the holding has been accurately formulated and its parameters considered.* It is not uncommon for attorneys and legal scholars to differ as to exactly what an opinion holds when attempting to justify (or negate) its application to subsequent legal controversy. Thus, the holding of any particular case should not be viewed as a static concept. However, each opinion placed in the casebook will represent at least one principle of law upon which general agreement can be reached. *The holdings are the source of the issues which the student will be expected to extract from the hypotheticals and discuss on the final exams.* Significant facts which could be useful to a party arguing that the holding should be expanded or narrowed should be noted immediately beside the holding.

Only a few lines should be devoted to summarizing the court's *rationale* and any dictum which could be useful to the resolution of a similar issue or which suggests an independent proposition of law. Dictum is language in an opinion which is broader than that which was necessary to decide the particular legal controversy before the court. Dictum becomes important when one is contending that a prior decision should be given an expansive or restrictive interpretation. This term will be explained more completely later.

Finally, it is not necessary to transcribe under the rationale the cases, Restatement sections or other authorities cited by the court in its decision. Grounds such as these should be reduced to single words such as *precedent* or *Restatement*. It is important, however, to understand the logic which underlies a decision in order to be able to argue that the same reasoning should (or should not) be applied to a slightly different set of circumstances.

Examples of Conventional and Capsule Briefs

The foregoing comments can probably be best understood by setting forth a few cases, and then analyzing briefs of them under the conventional method as well as along the lines suggested above. The first opinion was excerpted from a widely used Torts casebook, entitled *Torts, Cases and Materials*.*

KATKO v. *BRINEY*

MOORE, C. J. The primary issue presented here is whether an owner may protect personal property in an unoccupied boarded-up farm house against trespassers

---

* W. Prosser and J. Wade, *Torts, Cases and Materials*, 5th Ed. (Foundation Press, 1971).

and thieves by a spring gun capable of inflicting death
or serious injury.

We are not here concerned with a man's right to protect his home and members of his family. Defendants'
home was several miles from the scene of the incident
to which we refer infra.

Plaintiff's action is for damages resulting from serious injury caused by a shot from a 20-gauge spring
shotgun set by defendants in a bedroom of an old farm
house which had been uninhabited for several years.
Plaintiff and his companion * * * had broken and entered the house to find and steal old bottles and dated
fruit jars which they considered antiques. * * *

The jury returned a verdict for plaintiff and against
defendants for $20,000 actual and $10,000 punitive
damages.

After careful consideration of defendants' motions
for judgment notwithstanding the verdict and for new
trial, the experienced and capable trial judge over-
ruled them and entered judgment on the verdict. Thus
we have this appeal by defendants. * * *

[The house was inherited from Mrs. Briney's grand-
parents and had been unoccupied for some time. There
had been a series of intrusions.] Defendants through
the years boarded up the windows and doors in an attempt to stop the intrusions. They had posted "no trespass" signs on the land several years before 1967. The
nearest one was 35 feet from the house. On June 11,
1967 defendants set "a shotgun trap" in the north bedroom. After Mr. Briney cleaned and oiled his 20-gauge
shotgun, the power of which he was well aware, defendants took it to the old house where they secured
it to an iron bed with the barrel pointed at the bedroom door. It was rigged with wire from the doorknob

to the gun's trigger so it would fire when the door was opened. Briney first pointed the gun so an intruder would be hit in the stomach but at Mrs. Briney's suggestion it was lowered to hit the legs. He admitted he did so "because I was mad and tired of being tormented" but "he did not intend to injure anyone." He gave no explanation of why he used a loaded shell and set it to hit a person already in the house. Tin was nailed over the bedroom window. The spring gun could not be seen from the outside. No warning of its presence was posted. * * *

[Plaintiff] entered the old house by removing a board from a porch window which was without glass. * * * As he started to open the north bedroom door the shotgun went off striking him in the right leg above the ankle bone. Much of his leg, including part of the tibia, was blown away. Only by * * * assistance was plaintiff able to get out of the house and after crawling some distance was put in his vehicle and rushed to a doctor and then to a hospital. He remained in the hospital 40 days. * * *

There was undenied medical testimony plaintiff had a permanent deformity, a loss of tissue, and a shortening of the leg. * * *

The main thrust of defendants' defense in the trial court and on this appeal is that "the law permits use of a spring gun in a dwelling or warehouse for the purpose of preventing the unlawful entry of a burglar or thief." * * *

*Instruction 6 stated: "An owner of premises is prohibited from willfully or intentionally injuring a trespasser by means of force that either takes life or inflicts great bodily injury; and therefore a person owning a premise is prohibited from setting out 'spring guns' and like dangerous devices which will likely take life or inflict great bodily injury, for the purpose of harming trespassers. The fact that the trespasser may be acting in violation of the law does not change the rule. The only time when such conduct of setting a 'spring gun' or a like dangerous device is justified would be when the trespasser was committing a felony of violence or a felony punishable by death, or where the trespasser was endangering human life by his act." * * *

The overwhelming weight of authority, both textbook and case law, supports the trial court's statement of the applicable principles of law. * * *

Restatement of Torts, section 85, page 180, states: "The value of human life and limb, not only to the individual concerned but also to society, so outweighs the interest of a possessor of land in excluding from it those whom he is not willing to admit thereto that a possessor of land has, as is stated in § 79, no privilege to use force intended or likely to cause death or serious harm against another whom the possessor sees about to enter his premises or meddle with his chattel, unless the intrusion threatens death or serious bodily harm to the occupiers or users of the premises. * * * A possessor of land cannot do indirectly and by a mechanical device that which, were he present, he could not do immediately and in person. Therefore, he cannot gain a privilege to install, for the purpose of protecting his land from intrusions harmless to the lives and limbs of the occupiers or users of it, a mechanical device whose only purpose is to inflict death or serious harm upon such as may intrude, by giving notice of his intention to inflict, by mechanical means and indirectly, harm which he could not, even after request, inflict directly were he present." * * *

The facts in Allison v. Fixcus, 156 Ohio St. 120, N.E.2d 237, decided in 1951, are very similar to the case at bar. There plaintiff's right to damages was recognized for injuries received when he feloniously broke a door latch and started to enter defendant's warehouse with intent to steal. As he entered a trap of two sticks of dynamite buried under the doorway by defendant owner was set off and plaintiff seriously injured. The court held the question whether a particular trap was justified as a use of reasonable and necessary force against a trespasser engaged in the commission of a felony should have been submitted to the jury. The Ohio Supreme Court recognized plaintiff's right to recover punitive or exemplary damages in addition to compensatory damages. * * *

In addition to civil liability many jurisdictions hold a landowner criminally liable for serious injuries or homicide caused by spring guns or other set devices. [Citations omitted.] * * *

The classic freshman brief of the foregoing case would probably resemble the following:

KATKO v. BRINEY

Facts—Plaintiff, a potential thief, was shot and seriously wounded by a spring gun while trying to break into defendants' unused farm house. Defendants had been robbed several times before, and had intentionally positioned this firearm to discharge upon anyone illegally attempting to gain entrance into a room in the farm house. Plaintiff brought suit and recovered a judgment of $30,000.00.

Procedure—Plaintiff won in the trial court, defendants have appealed to the Supreme Court of the state.

Issue—Is a landowner liable to a trespasser for wounds suffered by the latter from a spring gun while attempting to burglarize an unused dwelling?

Holding—A landowner or occupier who positions a spring gun so that it will fire and inflict serious injury upon a trespasser who is attempting to burglarize his unused farm house is liable to the trespasser for injuries suffered thereby.

Rationale—The value of human life outweighs the interest which a property owner has in excluding others from his premises, Section 85 of the Restatement of Torts.

It should be noted at the outset that the foregoing brief requires almost a full page of handwritten notes to summarize two and one-half pages of text. If this ratio were maintained throughout the casebook, a student would have about 350 pages of briefs (plus classnotes) to review for the Torts final alone. The infeasibility of such a result should be self-evident. The facts, procedure and issue portions of briefed opinions will rarely be incorporated into the *syntheses,* which will be discussed shortly. More significant, however, is that the legal principle which *Katko* v. *Briney* was placed in the casebook to illustrate has *not* been accurately stated, with the consequence that the potential issue represented by this case may not be recognized when it appears on the exam hypotheticals. The over-all effect is that this brief is only of minimal effectiveness for review or test purposes.

If the suggestions for summarizing a case discussed

earlier in this chapter had been adopted, the result would be the following capsule brief:

KATKO v. BRINEY

H (Holding)—One cannot utilize devices which cause serious bodily injury to another in defense of property (not a home or business) (no warning posted).

R (Rationale)—Human life is more important than property.

It is submitted that the foregoing three lines are all that is required to capsulize this decision. Facts which, if present, *might* have resulted in a different ruling are noted immediately after the holding. The opinion does not expressly state that if the spring gun had been placed in a dwelling, or if signs warning of serious injury if illegal entry is attempted had been posted, the landowner would have prevailed. However, such a conclusion could be inferred from the way in which the court expressly stated that these factors were absent. The procedural setting was irrelevant and therefore is omitted. The holding accurately reflects the principle of law which *Katko* v. *Briney* was intended to illustrate, and also indicates the issue which the court considered. The crux of the court's rationale is noted in a single line.

Probably, the most common briefing error committed by freshmen is to state the holding too narrowly (i.e., placing excessive emphasis upon the particular facts, as opposed to the broader principle of law which the opinion represents). The traditional brief illustrates this mistake. The fact that a spring gun was utilized, and the injury was inflicted in defense of a farm house, are insignificant in themselves. If the trespasser had been seriously injured by stepping into a concealed pitfall which had been dug across the entrance to a vegetable patch the holding and rationale would have been exactly the same. Similarly, if a trespasser were seriously injured by a specially trained dog while trying to break into a car in which the animal had deliberately been left, the applicable principle of law would be the same. The crucial point which *Katko* v. *Briney* was placed in the casebook to illustrate is the proposition that one person cannot expose another human being to serious injury merely in the defense of property.

The reader should not be discouraged if several rereadings are necessary to extract the correct holding. My associate advisor at Columbia stated that he did not feel he knew a case until it had been read at least three times. The ability to formulate accurate holdings is a skill which may take a substantial period of time to develop. In no event, however, should a student yield to the temptation of simply transcribing substantial portions of an opinion into his brief. Such non-thinking, time-consuming condensations are of little true academic benefit.

Consideration of Completed Briefs

After a student is satisfied that he or she has grasped the principle of law and the underlying logic which the opinion represents, a considerable amount of time should be spent in contemplating the applicability of the holding and rationale to other circumstances. For example, would the outcome of *Katko* v. *Briney* have been different (the trespasser would *not* have prevailed) if the landowner had posted a notice which warned that lethal devices had been set in the house? How conspicuous would such a sign have to be? What if the sign was visible during the day, but not in the evening hours when the injury occurred? What if the structure which had been invaded was a *temporarily* vacant dwelling or factory (over a weekend, or overnight, for instance)? The rationale of *Katko* v. *Briney*, that human life occupies a higher place in our system of values than material possessions, suggests that under no circumstances can one lawfully put forces in motion which could inflict physical injury upon another in defense of property. Therefore, the fact that a warning sign was posted, or that a temporarily unoccupied dwelling or factory was involved, would not appear to justify a different result. In fact, the logic of this decision carried to its extreme would lead to the conclusion that a property owner could never use force against a trespasser (provided the latter makes no assault directly upon him), even though the burglary is occurring right before his eyes.

On the other hand, if a warning is posted and the trespasser still chooses to proceed, isn't the primary responsibility for the ensuing injury his own? Also, wouldn't the installation of a spring gun for the protection of one's home or business premises stand on an entirely different footing than that of an unused farm house? In the former instance, one is protecting what is sometimes considered an extension of one's very self; in the latter, the source of one's livelihood. Finally, what is *serious* injury? If the mechanism or force which the property owner set into motion simply broke the intruder's leg (as opposed to causing permanent injury), would the former be free from liability? What if a permanent injury was not intended, but nevertheless occurred?

The viability of the holding and rationale should also be considered. Despite the court's decision in *Katko* v. *Briney*,

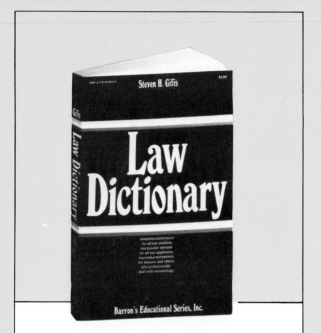

Author: STEVEN H. GIFIS, Assoc. Professor of Law
Rutgers, State Univ. of New Jersey, School of Law/Newark

Law Dictionary includes over 1500 legal words, phrases, and expressions frequently used in first-year law courses on: civil procedure, commercial law and contracts, constitutional law, criminal law and procedure, real and personal property, and torts. All definitions are clear, concise, technically accurate, and up-to-date.

- Definitions drawn from cases or other authority
- Entries thoroughly documented with citations for further research
- Latin expressions defined, with pronunciations

ORDER FORM

Barron's Educational Series, Inc.
113 Crossways Park Drive
Woodbury, New York 11797

Please send the quantities indicated below:
Quantity

_____ **Law Dictionary,** By Steven H. Gifis, 352 pages, $2.95 paper

_____ **How to Succeed in Law School,** By Brian Siegel, 272 pages, $2.95 paper

_____ **The President and Congress: Toward a New Power Balance,** By James W. Davis and Delbert Ringquist, 240 pages, $2.50 paper

_____ **The Law, The Supreme Court and the People's Rights,** By Ann Fagan Ginger, 720 pages, $3.95 paper, $10.95 cloth

_____ **The Meaning of the Constitution,** by Angela R. Holder, 110 pages, $2.25 paper, $6.25 cloth

_____ **Essentials of Political Parties: Their Relation to American Government,** by Samuel A. Johnson, 204 pages, $1.95 paper

_____ **Essentials of American Government,** by Ernst B. Schulz, 671 pages, $3.95 paper, $9.00 cloth

_____ **National Conventions: Nominations Under the Big Top,** James Davis, 156 pages, $1.50 pa.

_____ **The Politics of Urbanism: The New Federalism,** by George Benson, 144 pages, $1.50 paper.

_____ **Politics of People-Power: Interest Groups and Lobbies in New York State,** by Joseph G. Metz, 112 pages, $1.50 paper

_____ **Corporations and Social Change,** by William Withers, 160 pages, $1.50 paper

_____ **Pressures Upon Congress,** by Thomas P. Murphy, 160 pages, $1.50 paper

_____ **Does the Citizen Stand a Chance? Politics of a State Legislature: New York,** by Peter A. A. Berle, 150 pages, $1.50 paper

All prices subject to change without notice. Usual discounts apply. If order amounts to $25 or less, please enclose check or money order. On all orders add 8% transportation charges. Add sales tax where applicable.

Name _____

Address _____

City _____

State _____ Zip _____

2432-2/76-10M

it could legitimately be contended that one should have the right to utilize dangerous devices to protect his private property from pillage (especially when the law enforcement authorities have been unable to prevent such encroachments on prior occasions). Must one sit by helplessly as his hard-earned possessions are filched because it is impossible to employ someone or personally be at each location where the property is located? Shouldn't a trespasser who is committing an illegal act bear the risk of any type of injury which results when his efforts are aborted? *It is important to remember that no opinion is sacrosanct and that its vitality is always subject to challenge.* In an examination the writer will usually be expected to be capable of arguing that adverse precedent does not represent *good* law, and therefore should not be followed.

Undertaking the mental exercises described above is crucial: first, it heightens your understanding of the potential extensions and limitations of legal principles; second, it develops your ability to argue each side of an issue. The former will help you to recognize the issues, the latter to discuss them. It should be pointed out that it is not necessary for you to resolve the questions which you conjure up when considering a holding in the sense of giving a positive or negative reply. It is essential, however, for test purposes that you acquire a feel for the arguments which could be made as new considerations come into play, and why such factual variations might bring about a different result.

There are several aids which a student can utilize to assure himself that the holding which has been formulated is substantially correct. First, the word or words which comprise the title of the subchapter in which the case is found will often be contained in the holding. For example, *Katko* v. *Briney* was included within a subchapter entitled "Defense of Property." An opinion is, after all, placed within a specific portion of a casebook precisely because it demonstrates an aspect of law within the purview of the subdivision heading. The commentary or casenotes immediately after an opinion in a casebook often suggest the legal principle which has just been illustrated. Classroom lectures and discussions with colleagues should also reveal the degree of expertise you have achieved in extracting the legal principle embodied in a case. Finally, many of the casebook opinions are cited in hornbooks, which usually have a *case index*. If the casebook opinion is listed in such an index, you can find the page on which the case was alluded to and for what proposition of law.

Other Examples of Conventional and Capsule Briefs

Because the ability to extract and formulate the legal principle contained in each opinion is the touchstone of the *checklist method*, another example is warranted. It is suggested that the reader try his or her hand at briefing the next case, *before* going over the comments which follow. The following opinion was taken from the Contracts' casebook which I used in law school, *Contracts, Cases and Materials*.*

LUCY v. ZEHMER

BUCHANAN, JUSTICE. This suit was instituted by W. O. Lucy and J. C. Lucy, complainants, against A. H. Zehmer and Ida S. Zehmer, his wife, defendants,

---

* Jones, Farnsworth, and Young, *Contracts, Cases and Materials*, (Foundation Press, 1965).

to have specific performance of a contract by which it was alleged the Zehmers had sold to W. O. Lucy a tract of land owned by A. H. Zehmer in Dinwiddie county containing 471.6 acres, more or less, known as the Ferguson farm, for $50,000. J. C. Lucy, the other complainant, is a brother of W. O. Lucy, to whom W. O. Lucy transferred a half interest in his alleged purchase.

The instrument sought to be enforced was written by A. H. Zehmer on December 20, 1952, in these words: "We hereby agree to sell to W. O. Lucy the Ferguson Farm complete for $50,000.00, title satisfactory to buyer," and signed by the defendants, A. H. Zehmer and Ida S. Zehmer.

The answer of A. H. Zehmer admitted that at the time mentioned W. O. Lucy offered him $50,000 cash for the farm, but that he, Zehmer, considered that the offer was made in jest; that so thinking, and both he and Lucy having had several drinks, he wrote out "the memorandum" quoted above and induced his wife to sign it; that he did not deliver the memorandum to Lucy, but that Lucy picked it up, read it, put it in his pocket, attempted to offer Zehmer $5 to bind the bargain, which Zehmer refused to accept, and realizing for the first time that Lucy was serious, Zehmer assured him that he had no intention of selling the farm and that the whole matter was a joke. Lucy left the premises insisting that he had purchased the farm.

Depositions were taken and the decree appealed from was entered holding that the complainants had failed to establish their right to specific performance, and dismissing their bill. The assignment of error is to this action of the court.

The defendants insist that the evidence was ample

to support their contention that the writing sought to be enforced was prepared as a bluff or dare to force Lucy to admit that he did not have $50,000; that the whole matter was a joke; that the writing was not delivered to Lucy and no binding contract was ever made between the parties.

It is an unusual, if not bizarre, defense. When made to the writing admittedly prepared by one of the defendants and signed by both, clear evidence is required to sustain it.

In his testimony Zehmer claimed that he "was high as a Georgia pine," and that the transaction "was just a bunch of two doggoned drunks bluffing to see who could talk the biggest and say the most." That claim is inconsistent with his attempt to testify in great detail as to what was said and what was done. It is contradicted by other evidence as to the condition of both parties, and rendered of no weight by the testimony of his wife that when Lucy left the restaurant she suggested that Zehmer drive him home. The record is convincing that Zehmer was not intoxicated to the extent of being unable to comprehend the nature and consequences of the instrument he executed, and hence that instrument is not to be invalidated on that ground. 17 C.J.S. Contracts, § 133, b., p. 483; Taliaferro v. Emery, 124 Va. 674, 98 S.E. 627. It was in fact conceded by defendants' counsel in oral argument that under the evidence Zehmer was not too drunk to make a valid contract.

The evidence is convincing also that Zehmer wrote two agreements, the first one beginning "I hereby agree to sell." Zehmer first said he could not remember about that, then that "I don't think I wrote but one out." Mrs. Zehmer said that what he wrote was "I hereby agree," but that the "I" was changed to "We" after that night. The agreement that was written and signed is in the record and indicates no such change. Neither are the mistakes in spelling that Zehmer sought to point out readily apparent.

The appearance of the contract, the fact that it was under discussion for forty minutes or more before it was signed; Lucy's objection to the first draft because it was written in the singular, and he wanted Mrs. Zehmer to sign it also; the rewriting to meet that objection and the signing by Mrs. Zehmer; the discussion of what was to be included in the sale, the provision for the examination of the title, the completeness of the instrument that was executed, the taking possession of it by Lucy with no request or suggestion by either of the defendants that he give it back, are facts which furnish persuasive evidence that the execution of the contract was a serious business transaction rather than a casual, jesting matter as defendants now contend. . . .

If it be assumed, contrary to what we think the evidence shows, that Zehmer was jesting about selling his farm to Lucy and that the transaction was intended by him to be a joke, nevertheless the evidence shows that Lucy did not so understand it but considered it to be a serious business transaction and the contract to be binding on the Zehmers as well as on himself. The very next day he arranged with his brother to put up half the money and take a half interest in the land. The day after that he employed an attorney to examine the title. The next night, Tuesday, he was back at Zehmer's place and there Zehmer told him for the first time, Lucy said, that he wasn't going to sell and he told Zehmer, "You know you sold that place fair and square." After receiving the report from his attorney that the title was good he wrote to Zehmer that he was ready to close the deal.

Not only did Lucy actually believe, but the evidence shows he was warranted in believing, that the contract represented a serious business transaction and a good faith sale and purchase of the farm.

In the field of contracts, as generally elsewhere, "We must look to the outward expression of a person as manifesting his intention rather than to his secret and unexpressed intention. 'The law imputes to a person an intention corresponding to the reasonable meaning of his words and acts.' First Nat. Exchange Bank of Roanoke v. Roanoke Oil Co., 169 Va. 99, 114, 192 S.E. 764, 770.

At no time prior to the execution of the contract had Zehmer indicated to Lucy by word or act that he was not in earnest about selling the farm. They had argued about it and discussed its terms, as Zehmer admitted, for a long time. Lucy testified that if there was any jesting it was about paying $50,000 that night. The contract and the evidence show that he was not expected to pay the money that night. Zehmer said that after the writing was signed he laid it down on the counter in front of Lucy. Lucy said Zehmer handed it to him. In any event there had been what appeared to be a good faith offer and a good faith acceptance, followed by the execution and apparent delivery of a written contract. Both said that Lucy put the writing in his pocket and then offered Zehmer $5 to seal the bargain. Not until then, even under the defendant's evidence, was anything said or done to indicate that the matter was a joke. Both of the Zehmers testified that when Zehmer asked his wife to sign he whispered that it was a joke so Lucy wouldn't hear and that it was not intended that he should hear.

The mental assent of the parties is not requisite for the formation of a contract. If the words or other acts of one of the parties have but one reasonable meaning, his undisclosed intention is immaterial except when an unreasonable meaning which he attaches to his manifestations is known to the other party. Restatement of the Law of Contracts, Vol. I, § 71, p. 74. . . .

An agreement or mutual assent is of course essential to a valid contract but the law imputes to a person an intention corresponding to the reasonable meaning of his words and acts. If his words and acts, judged by a reasonable standard, manifest an intention to agree, it is immaterial what may be the real but unexpressed state of his mind. 17 C.J.S., Contracts, § 32, p. 361; 12 Am.Jur., Contracts, § 19, p. 515.

So a person cannot set up that he was merely jesting when his conduct and words would warrant a reasonable person in believing that he intended a real agreement. . . .

Whether the writing signed by the defendants and now sought to be enforced by the complainants was the result of a serious offer by Lucy and a serious acceptance by the defendants, or was a serious offer by Lucy and an acceptance in secret jest by the defendants, in either event it constituted a binding contract of sale between the parties. . . .

The complainants are entitled to have specific performance of the contract sued on. The decree appealed from is therefore reversed and the cause is remanded for the entry of a proper decree requiring the defendants to perform the contract in accordance with the prayer of the bill.

The typical freshman brief of *Lucy* v. *Zehmer* based upon the conventional method would probably resemble the following:

LUCY v. ZEHMER

Facts—The Zehmers executed a writing which purported to sell certain real property to the Lucys. Mr. Zehmer contended that at the time he made the writing he did not think Lucy was serious and that both parties were intoxicated. However, the parties did discuss the terms for about forty minutes, Lucy acted upon the purported contract in good faith, and Zehmer did permit Lucy to take actual physical possession of the writing.

Procedure—Lucy brought an action for specific performance against Zehmer. The lower court held that Lucy had failed to establish his right to specific performance and dismissed their suit. The Lucys have appealed.

Issue—Is an offer which is purportedly made in jest and while intoxicated binding upon the offeree, where the offeree reasonably believes that the offeror was serious at the time the contract was accepted?

Holding—It is not a defense to a contract that one was merely jesting when that party's words and conduct would reasonably lead the offeree to believe a real agreement was intended.

Rationale—The law imputes to a person an intention corresponding to the reasonable meaning of his words and acts, regardless of what his undisclosed intentions might be; Restatement of Contracts.

Again, the foregoing brief contains much information

which is unnecessary for exam purposes. The essence of the opinion is the holding. The facts, procedure and issue segments are extraneous for exam purposes. The policy behind the court's rationale is never stated in the decision. While the formulation of the holding of this case is not technically incorrect, the principle of law represented by *Lucy* v. *Zehmer* should be stated in somewhat broader terms. This decision would certainly be applicable to the situation where an offer is *accepted* in jest, or where an offeror states a figure for which he would sell something (be it real or personal property) merely for the actual purpose of obtaining an estimation of its value. Therefore, a preferable statement of the holding would simply be: "A party's intentions are determined by his outward expressions."

Lucy v. *Zehmer* also mentioned two possible defenses to the enforcement of a contract which, though not applicable in this instance, should be noted for possible further reference. They were (1) intoxication to the extent that one is not capable of understanding the legal consequences of his actions,* and (2) awareness by one party of the other's unexpressed intentions. The court's comments about drunkenness as a defense is an example of dictum. This statement was not necessary to the decision since counsel for the Zehmers had admitted his client "was not too drunk to make a valid contract." Thus, in a subsequent case the party seeking to avoid an agreement made while inebriated would cite *Lucy* v. *Zehmer* as authority for the proposition that such contracts are invalid, while his adversary would point out that this issue was never squarely considered by the court in *Lucy* v. *Zehmer*.

---

* This statement is of dubious validity since one who is "high" in an unobstrusive manner will probably be responsible for any contractural commitments made during this period.

A brief of *Lucy* v. *Zehmer* along the lines suggested in this book would be the following:

H—A party's intentions are determined by his outward expressions (jokes), except where (1) he cannot comprehend the legal consequences of his actions, or (2) his undisclosed intention is known to the other party.

R—The reasonable expectations of a party should not be disappointed. (Although this was never explicitly articulated, it is a rationale which underlies much of Contracts' Law).

Of course, the next steps would be (1) application of the holding to different circumstances, and (2) consideration of the vigor of the principle of law which the holding represents.

Summary

It is hoped that by this time the reader has acquired a feeling for extracting and stating the holding and rationale of a case in a terse, but efficient manner. If you have several hundred pages of briefs to review when commencing preparation for finals your task will be hopeless. Several readings of an opinion will often be necessary to accomplish satisfactory results. Once the principle of law contained in an opinion is formulated it is absolutely essential to consider its implications and applicability to varied factual situations. *It is only after you UNDERSTAND the principle of law which is embodied in an opinion and its parameters have been considered that you will be likely to perceive its (1) interrelationship to the other materials, and (2) applicability to the hypotheticals which will appear on the final exam.*

In the motion picture *The Paper Chase*, which describes

the experiences of a first-year law student at Harvard, there is a brief dialogue in which the central character, who ultimately excels academically, is stopped in a hallway by a classmate and asked to recall the facts of a particular case. The former answers, "Don't worry about the facts, just remember *fundamental breach* [a doctrine of Contracts' law]." This is the essence of the point which I have tried to make on the foregoing pages. For success on hypothetical-type exams a student must understand the proposition of law which the cases were intended to illustrate, and their potential applicability to different situations. You need not, and therefore should not, be concerned with drafting and memorizing extensive summaries of each opinion. The individual holdings are the basic components of syntheses, which are the subject of the following chapter.

The Synthesis

The Conventional Synthesis and a More Effective Synthesis

The term *synthesis* usually connotes a summary of an entire law course. Unfortunately, it is usually compiled near the end of the semester and represents little more than a mere stringing-together of important points of each brief in the order in which they appeared in the casebook. Such a mechanical, unthinking condensation does little to prepare you for the hypotheticals which will appear on finals. Actually, each subchapter and chapter should be synthesized as soon as completed. These mini-syntheses should, in turn, be subject to continuous addition, deletion and modification as new materials are learned. There should be a separate synthesis for each major area of a course. *The truly effective synthesis is one in which the materials of a course are arranged in the order in which the potential issues they represent would arise in a factual situation which contained every possible issue.* The key to creating a synthesis is recognizing the interrelationship (1) of the principles contained within each doctrine or topic of a course, and (2) between the various doctrines and topics (usually represented by chapter and subdivision headings) themselves.

An Example of Subchapter Synthesis

Step 1 in constructing a synthesis is to read and brief the materials contained within the initial subdivision of a chapter. In performing this task it is important to keep in mind that, generally speaking, each opinion has been placed in the casebook to demonstrate a particular proposition of law. Occasionally, however, two or more opinions may deal with a single proposition of law or criterion so that the student can acquire a feel for the manner in which it is applied in practice. Each opinion or other bit of information should add some new facet or twist, even if it is relatively minor, to the data which preceded it. *Reconciling these various opinions is the essence of synthesizing.* After you have extracted and assembled the pertinent information of the subchapter, classnotes and summaries of any other materials, you are ready to go on to the next step.

Step 2 is to devise a formulation which incorporates these materials in an organized, concise manner. Again, an illustration is probably the best means of explanation. The cases within the initial subchapter of Jones, Farnsworth and Young, *Contracts, Cases and Materials,* mentioned earlier, are reproduced on the following pages. The reader should brief these opinions before proceeding to the discussion which follows:

Contracts, Cases and Materials
Chapter 1
The Agreement Process
Section 1. The Offer

BALFOUR v. *BALFOUR*

Court of Appeal, 1919.
[1919] 2 K.B. 571.

The plaintiff sued the defendant (her husband) for money which she claimed to be due in respect of an agreed allowance of 30£ a month. The alleged agreement was entered into under the following circumstances. The parties were married in August, 1900. The husband, a civil engineer, had a post under the Government of Ceylon as Director of Irrigation, and after the marriage he and his wife went to Ceylon, and lived there together until the year 1915, except that in 1906 they paid a short visit to this country, and in 1908 the wife came to England in order to undergo an operation, after which she returned to Ceylon. In November, 1915, she came to this country with her husband, who was on leave. They remained in England until August, 1916, when the husband's leave was up and he had to return. The wife however on the doctor's advice remained in England. On August 8, 1916, the husband being about to sail, the alleged parol agreement sued upon was made. The plaintiff, as appeared from the judge's note, gave the following evidence of what took place: "In August, 1916, defendant's leave was up. I was suffering from rheumatic arthritis. The doctor advised my staying in England for some months, not to go out till November 4. On August 8 my husband sailed. He gave me a cheque from 8th to 31st for 24£, and promised to give me 30£ per month till I returned." Later on she said: "My husband and I wrote the figures together on August 8; 34£ shown. Afterward he said 30£." In cross-examination she said that they had not agreed to live apart until subsequent differences arose between them, and that the agreement of August, 1916, was one which might be made by a couple in amity. Her husband in consultation with her assessed her needs, and said he would send 30£ per month for her maintenance. She further said that she then understood that the defendant would be returning to England in a few months, but that he afterwards wrote to her suggesting that they had better remain apart. In March, 1918, she commenced proceedings for restitution of conjugal rights, and on July 30 she obtained a decree nisi. On December 16, 1918, she obtained an order for alimony.

Sargant, J. held that the husband was under an obligation to support his wife, and the parties had contracted that the extent of that obligation should be defined in terms of so much a month. The consent of the wife to that arrangement was a sufficient consideration to constitute a contract which could be sued upon.

He accordingly gave judgment for the plaintiff.

The husband appealed.

[The concurring opinions of Warrington, L. J., and Duke, L. J., are omitted.]

ATKIN, L. J. The defence to this action on the alleged contract is that the defendant, the husband, entered into no contract with his wife, and for the determination of that it is necessary to remember that there are agreements between parties which do not result in contracts within the meaning of that term in our law. The ordinary example is where two parties agree to take a walk together, or where there is an offer and an acceptance of hospitality. Nobody would suggest in ordinary circumstances that those agreements result in what we know as a contract, and one of the most usual forms of agreement which does not constitute a contract appears to me to be the arrangements which are made between husband and wife. It is quite common, and it is the natural and inevitable result of the relationship of husband and wife, that the two spouses should make arrangements between them-

selves—agreements such as are in dispute in this action—agreements for allowances, by which the husband
agrees that he will pay to his wife a certain sum of
money, per week, or per month, or per year, to cover
either her own expenses or the necessary expenses of
the household and of the children of the marriage, and
in which the wife promises either expressly or implied-
ly to apply the allowance for the purpose for which
it is given. To my mind those agreements, or many of
them, do not result in contracts at all, and they do not
result in contracts even though there may be what as
between other parties would constitute consideration
for the agreement. The consideration, as we know, may
consist either in some right, interest, profit or benefit
accruing to one party, or some forbearance, detriment,
loss or responsibility given, suffered or undertaken by
the other. That is a well-known definition, and it constantly happens, I think, that such arrangements made
between husband and wife are arrangements in which
there are mutual promises, or in which there is consideration in form within the definition that I have
mentioned. Nevertheless they are not contracts, and
they are not contracts because the parties did not intend that they should be attended by legal consequences.
To my mind it would be of the worst possible example
to hold that agreements such as this resulted in legal
obligations which could be enforced in the Courts. It
would mean this, that when the husband makes his wife
a promise to give her an allowance of 30s. or 2£ a
week, whatever he can afford to give her, for the maintenance of the household and children, and she promises so to apply it, not only could she sue him for his
failure in any week to supply the allowance, but he
could sue her for non-performance of the obligation,

express or implied, which she had undertaken upon her part. All I can say is that the small Courts of this country would have to be multiplied one hundredfold if these arrangements were held to result in legal obligations. They are not sued upon, not because the parties are reluctant to enforce their legal rights when the agreement is broken, but because the parties, in the inception of the arrangement, never intended that they should be sued upon. Agreements such as these are outside the realm of contracts altogether. The common law does not regulate the form of agreements between spouses. Their promises are not sealed with seals and sealing wax. The consideration that really obtains for them is that natural love and affection which counts for so little in these cold Courts. The terms may be repudiated, varied or renewed as performance proceeds or as disagreements develop, and the principles of the common law as to exoneration and discharge and accord and satisfaction are such as find no place in the domestic code. The parties themselves are advocates, judges, Courts, sheriff's officer and reporter. In respect of these promises each house is a domain into which the King's writ does not seek to run, and to which his officers do not seek to be admitted. The only question in this case is whether or not this promise was of such a class or not. For the reasons given by my brethern it appears to me to be plainly established that the promise here was not intended by either party to be attended by legal consequences. I think the onus was upon the plaintiff, and the plaintiff has not established any contract. The parties were living together, the wife intending to return. The suggestion is that the husband bound himself to pay 30£ a month under all circumstances, and she bound herself to be satisfied with that

sum under all circumstances, and, although she was in
ill-health and alone in this country, that out of that
sum she undertook to defray the whole of the medical
expenses that might fall upon her, whatever might be
the development of her illness, and in whatever expenses it might involve her. To my mind neither party
contemplated such a result. I think that the parol evidence upon which the case turns does not establish a
contract. I think that the letters do not evidence such
a contract, or amplify the oral evidence which was
given by the wife, which is not in dispute. For these
reasons I think the judgment of the Court below was
wrong and that this appeal should be allowed.

Appeal allowed.

LUCY v. ZEHMER

.   .   .   .

CRAFT v. ELDER & JOHNSTON CO.

Court of Appeals of Ohio, Montgomery County, 1941.
38 N.E.2d 416

[Action by Craft against Elder & Johnston Co. for
alleged breach of contract. From a judgment of dismissal plaintiff appeals.]

BARNES, JUDGE. . . . On or about January 31, 1940,
the defendant, the Elder & Johnston Company, carried
an advertisement in the Dayton Shopping News, an
offer for sale of a certain all electric sewing machine
for the sum of $26 as a "Thursday Only Special."
Plaintiff in her petition, after certain formal allegations, sets out the substance of the above advertisement
carried by defendant in the Dayton Shopping News.

She further alleges that the above publication is an advertising paper distributed in Montgomery County and throughout the city of Dayton; that on Thursday, February 1, 1940, she tendered to the defendant company $26 in payment for one of the machines offered in the advertisement, but that defendant refused to fulfill the offer and has continued to so refuse. The petition further alleges that the value of the machine offered was $175 and she asks damages in the sum of $149 plus interest from February 1, 1940. . . .

The trial court dismissed plaintiff's petition as evidenced by a journal entry, the pertinent portion of which reads as follows: "Upon consideration the court finds that said advertisement was not an offer which could be accepted by plaintiff to form a contract, and this case is therefore dismissed with prejudice to a new action, at costs of plaintiff."

Within statutory time plaintiff filed notice of appeal on questions of law and thus lodged the case in our court. . . .

It seems to us that this case may easily be determined on well-recognized elementary principles. The first question to be determined is the proper characterization to be given to defendant's advertisement in the Shopping News. . . .

"It is clear that in the absence of special circumstances an ordinary newspaper advertisement is not an offer, but is an offer to negotiate—an offer to receive offers—or, as it is sometimes called, an offer to chaffer." Restatement of the Law of Contracts, Par. 25, Page 31.

Under the above paragraph the following illustration is given, " 'A', a clothing merchant, advertises overcoats of a certain kind for sale at $50. This is not an offer but an invitation to the public to come and purchase."

"Thus, if goods are advertised for sale at a certain price, it is not an offer and no contract is formed by the statement of an intending purchaser that he will take a specified quantity of the goods at that price. The construction is rather favored that such an advertisement is a mere invitation to enter into a bargain rather than an offer. So a published price list is not an offer to sell the goods listed at the published price." Williston on Contracts, Revised Edition, Vol. 1, Par. 27, Pages 54.

"The commonest example of offers meant to open negotiations and to call forth offers in the technical sense are advertisements, circulars and trade letters sent out by business houses. While it is possible that the offers made by such means may be in such form as to become contracts, they are often merely expressions of a willingness to negotiate." Page on the Law Contracts, 2d Ed., Vol. 1, Page 112, Par. 84.

"Business advertisements published in newspapers and circulars sent out by mail or distributed by hand stating that the advertiser has a certain quantity or quality of goods which he wants to dispose of at certain prices, are not offers which become contracts as soon as any person to whose notice they may come signifies his acceptance by notifying the other that he will take a certain quantity of them. They are merely invitations to all persons who may read them that the advertiser is ready to receive offers for the goods at the price stated." 13 Corpus Juris 289, Par. 97. . . .

We are constrained to the view that the trial court committed no prejudicial error in dismissing plaintiff's petition.

The judgment of the trial court will be affirmed and costs adjudged against the plaintiff-appellant.

LEFKOWITZ v. GREAT MINNEAPOLIS SURPLUS STORE, 251 Minn. 188, 86 N.W.2d 689 (1957). [The Great Minneapolis Surplus Store published the following advertisement in a Minneapolis newspaper:

"SATURDAY 9 A.M.
2 BRAND NEW PASTEL
MINK 3-SKIN SCARFS
Selling for $89.50
Out they go
Saturday. Each $1.00
1 BLACK LAPIN STOLE
Beautiful,
worth $139.50 ....$1.00
FIRST COME
FIRST SERVED"

Lefkowitz was the first to present himself on Saturday and demanded the Lapin stole for one dollar. The store refused to sell to him because of a "house rule" that the offer was intended for women only. Lefkowitz sued the store and was awarded $138.50 as damages. The store appealed.]

MURPHY, JUSTICE. . . . The defendant relies principally on Craft v. Elder & Johnston Co. . . . On the facts before us we are concerned with whether the advertisement constituted an offer, and, if so, whether the plaintiff's conduct constituted an acceptance. There are numerous authorities which hold that a particular advertisement in a newspaper or circular letter relating to a sale of articles may be construed by the court as constituting an offer, acceptance of which would complete a contract. . . . The test of whether a binding obligation may originate in advertisements addressed to the general public is "whether the facts show that some performance was promised in positive terms in return for something requested." 1 Williston, Contracts (rev. ed.) § 27. The authorities above cited emphasize that, where the offer is clear, definite and explicit, and leaves nothing open for negotiation, it constitutes an offer, acceptance of which will complete the contract. . . . Whether in any individual instance a newspaper advertisement is an offer rather than an invitation to make an offer depends on the legal intention of the parties and the surrounding circumstances. . . . We are of the view on the facts before us that the offer by the defendant of the sale of the Lapin fur was clear, definite, and explicit, and left nothing open for negotiation. . . . The defendant contends that the offer was modified by a "house rule" to the effect that only women were qualified to receive the bargains advertised. The advertisement contained no such restriction. This objection may be disposed of briefly by stating that, while an advertiser has the right at any time before acceptance to modify his offer, he does not have the right, after acceptance, to impose new or arbitrary conditions not contained in the published offer. . . .

Affirmed.

OWEN v. TUNISON

Supreme Judicial Court of Maine, 1932
131 Me. 42, 158 A. 926.

Action by W. H. Owen against R. G. Tunison for breach of contract.

BARNES, J. This case is reported to the law court, and such judgment is to be rendered as the law and the admissible evidence require.

Plaintiff charges that defendant agreed in writing to sell him the Bradley block and lot, situated in Bucksport, for a stated price in cash, that he later refused to perfect the sale, and that plaintiff, always willing and ready to pay the price, has suffered loss on account of defendant's unjust refusal to sell, and claims damages.

From the record it appears that defendant, a resident of Newark, N. J., was, in the fall of 1929, the owner of the Bradley block and lot.

With the purpose of purchasing, on October 23, 1929, plaintiff wrote the following letter:

"Dear Mr. Tunison:

"Will you sell me your store property which is located on Main St. in Bucksport, Me. running from Montgomery's Drug Store on one corner to a Grocery Store on the other, for the sum of $6,000.00?"

Nothing more of this letter need be quoted.

On December 5, following, plaintiff received defendant's reply, apparently written in Cannes, France, on November 12, and it reads:

"In reply to your letter of Oct. 23rd which has been forwarded to me in which you inquire about the Bradley Block, Bucksport, Me.

"Because of improvements which have been added and an expenditure of several thousand dollars it would not be possible for me to sell it unless I was to receive $16,000.00 cash.

"The upper floors have been converted into apartments with baths and the b'l'dg put into first class condition.

"Very truly yours,

"[Signed] R. G. Tunison."

Whereupon, and at once, plaintiff sent to defendant, and the latter received, in France, the following message:

"Accept your offer for Bradley block Bucksport Terms sixteen thousand cash send deed to Eastern Trust and Banking Co Bangor Maine Please acknowledge."

Four days later he was notified that defendant did not wish to sell the property, and on the 14th day of January following brought suit for his damages.

Granted that damages may be due a willing buyer if the owner refuses to tender a deed of real estate, after the latter has made an offer in writing to sell to the former, and such offer has been so accepted, it remains for us to point out that defendant here is not shown to have written to plaintiff an offer to sell.

There can have been no contract for the sale of the property desired, no meeting of the minds of the owner and prospective purchaser, unless there was an offer or proposal of sale. It cannot be successfully argued that defendant made any offer or proposal of sale.

In a recent case the words, "Would not consider less than half" is held "not to be taken as an outright offer to sell for one-half." Sellers v. Warren, 116 Me. 350, 102 A. 40, 41.

Where an owner of millet seed wrote, "I want $2.25 per cwt. for this seed f. o. b. Lowell," in an action for damages for alleged breach of contract to sell at the figure quoted above, the court held: "He [defendant] does not say, 'I offer to sell to you.' The language used is general, and such as may be used in an advertisement, or circular addressed generally to those engaged in the seed business, and is not an offer by which he may be bound, if accepted, by any or all of the persons addressed." Nebraska Seed Co. v. Harsh, 98 Neb. 89, 152 N.W. 310, 311, and cases cited in note L.R.A. 1915F, 824.

Defendant's letter of December 5 in response to an offer of $6,000 for his property may have been written with the intent to open negotiations that might lead to a sale. It was not a proposal to sell.

Judgment for defendant.

HARVEY v. FACEY, [1893] A. C. 552 (P.C.)

(Jamaica). [Harvey and another were interested in a piece of property known as Bumper Hall Pen. Facey, the owner, had been engaged in negotiations for its sale to the town of Kingston. Harvey telegraphed Facey, who was on a journey, "Will you sell us Bumper Hall Pen? Telegraph lowest cash price—answer paid." Facey replied by telegram, "Lowest price for Bumper Hall Pen £900." Harvey answered, "We agree to buy Bumper Hall Pen for the sum of nine hundred pounds asked by you." Harvey sued for specific performance of this agreement and for an injunction to restrain the town of Kingston from taking a conveyance of the property. The trial court dismissed the action on the ground that the agreement did not disclose a concluded contract; the Supreme Court of Jamaica reversed; the defendants appealed to the Judicial Committee of the Privy Council.]

LORD MORRIS. . . . [T]heir Lordships concur in the judgment of Mr. Justice Curran that there was no concluded contract between the appellants and L. M. Facey to be collected from the aforesaid telegrams. The first telegram asks two questions. The first question is as to the willingness of L. M. Facey to sell to the appellants [i.e. Harvey]; the second question asks the lowest price, and the word "telegraph" is in its collocation addressed to that second question only. L. M. Facey replied to the second question only, and gives his lowest price. The third telegram from the appellants treats the answer of L. M. Facey stating his lowest price as an unconditional offer to sell to them at the price named. Their Lordships cannot treat the telegram from L. M. Facey as binding him in any respect, except to the extent it does by its term, viz., the lowest price. Everything else is left open, and the reply telegram from the appellants cannot be treated as an acceptance of an offer to sell to them; it is an offer that required to be accepted by L. M. Facey. The contract could only be completed if L. M. Facey had accepted the appellants' last telegram. It has been contended for the appellants that L. M. Facey's telegram should be read as saying "yes" to the first question put in the appellants' telegram, but there is nothing to support that contention. L. M. Facey's telegram gives a precise answer to a precise question, viz., the price. The contract must appear by the telegrams, whereas the appellants are obliged to contend that an acceptance of the first question is to be implied. Their Lordships are of opinion that the mere statement of the lowest price at which the vendor would sell contains no implied contract to sell at that price to the persons making the inquiry. . . . [Reversed and the judgment of the trial court restored.]

FAIRMOUNT GLASS WORKS v. CRUNDEN-MARTIN WOODENWARE CO.

Court of Appeals of Kentucky, 1899.
106 Ky. 659, 51 S.W. 196, 21 Ky. Law Rep. 264.
Action by the Crunden-Martin Woodenware Company against the Fairmount Glass Works to recover damages for breach of contract. Judgment for plaintiff, and defendant appeals. Affirmed.

HOBSON, J. On April 20, 1895, appellee wrote appellant the following letter:

"St. Louis, Mo., April 20, 1895. Gentlemen: Please advise us the lowest price you can make us on our order for ten car loads of Mason green jars, complete, with caps, packed one dozen in a case, either delivered here, or f. o. b. cars your place, as you prefer. State terms and cash discount. Very truly, Crunden-Martin W. W. Co."

To this letter appellant answered as follows:

"Fairmount, Ind. April 23, 1895. Crunden-Martin Wooden Ware Co., St. Louis, Mo.—Gentlemen: Replying to your favor of April 20, we quote you Mason fruit jars, complete, in one-dozen boxes, delivered in East St. Louis, Ill.: Pints, $4.50, quarts, $5.00, half gallons, $6.50 per gross, for immediate acceptance, and shipment not later than May 15, 1895; sixty days' acceptance, or 2 off, cash in ten days. Your truly, Fairmount Glass Works.

"Please note that we make all quotations and contracts subject to the contingencies of agencies or transportation, delays or accidents beyond our control."

For reply thereto, appellee sent the following telegrams on April 24, 1895:

"Fairmount Glass Works, Fairmount, Ind.: Your letter twenty-third received. Enter order ten car loads as per your quotation. Specifications mailed. Crunden-Martin W. W. Co."

In response to this telegram, appellant sent the following:

"Fairmount, Ind., April 24, 1895. Crunden-Martin W. W. Co., St. Louis, Mo.: Impossible to book your order. Output all sold. See letter. Fairmount Glass Works."

Appellee insists that, by its telegram sent in answer to the letter of April 23d, the contract was closed for the purchase of 10 car loads of Mason fruit jars. Appellant insists that the contract was not closed by this telegram, and that it had the right to decline to fill the order at the time it sent its telegram of April 24. This is the chief question in the case. The court below gave judgment in favor of appellee, and appellant has appealed, earnestly insisting that the judgment is erroneous.

We are referred to a number of authorities holding that a quotation of prices is not an offer to sell, in the sense that a completed contract will arise out of the giving of an order for merchandise in accordance with the proposed terms. There are a number of cases holding that the transaction is not completed until the order so made is accepted. 7 Am. & Eng.Enc.Law (2d Ed.) p. 138; Smith v. Gowdy, 8 Allen, Mass., 566; Beaupre v. Telegraph Co., 21 Minn. 155. But each case must turn largely upon the language there used. In this case we think there was more than a quotation of prices, although appellant's letter uses the word "quote" in stating the prices given. The true meaning of the correspondence must be determined by reading it as a whole. Appellee's letter of April 20th, which began the transaction, did not ask for a quotation of prices. It reads: "Please advise us the lowest price you can make us on our order for ten carloads of Mason green jars. . . State terms and cash discount." From this appellant could not fail to understand that appellee wanted to know at what price it would sell ten car loads of these jars; so when, in answer, it wrote: "We quote you Mason fruit jars . . . pints $4.50, quarts $5.00, half gallons $6.50, per gross, for immediate acceptance; . . . 2 off, cash in ten days,"—it must be deemed as intending to give appellee the information it asked for. We can hardly understand what is meant by the words "for immediate acceptance," unless the latter was intended as a proposition to sell at these prices if accepted immediately. In construing every contract, the aim of the court is to arrive at the intention of the parties. In none of the cases to which we have been referred on behalf of appellant was there on the face of the correspondence any such expression of intention to make an offer to sell on the terms indicated. . . . The expression in appellant's letter, "for immediate acceptance," taken in connection with appellee's letter, in effect, at what price it would sell it the goods, is, it seems to us, much stronger evidence of a present offer, which, when accepted immediately, closed the contract. Appellee's letter was plainly an inquiry for the price and terms on which appellant would sell it the goods, and appellant's answer to it was not a quotation of prices, but a definite offer to sell on the terms indicated, and could not be withdrawn after the terms had been accepted.

It will be observed that the telegram of acceptance refers to the specifications mailed. These specifications were contained in the following letter: "St. Louis, Mo., April 24, 1895. Fairmount Glass Works Co., Fairmount, Ind.—Gentlemen: We received your letter of 23rd this morning, and telegraphed you in reply as follows: 'Your letter 23rd received. Enter order ten car loads as per your quotation. Specifications mailed,'— which we now confirm. We have accordingly entered this contract on our books for the ten cars Mason green jars, complete, with caps and rubbers, one dozen in case, delivered to us in East St. Louis at $4.50 per gross for pint, $5.00 for quart, $6.50 for one-half gallon. Terms, 60 days' acceptance, or 2 per cent. for cash in ten days to be shipped no later than May 15, 1895. The jars and caps to be strictly first-quality goods. You may ship the first car to us here assorted: Five gross pint, fifty-five gross quart, forty gross one-half gallon. Specifications for the remaining 9 cars we will send later. Crunden-Martin W. W. Co." It is insisted for appellant that this was not an acceptance of the offer as made; that the stipulation "The jars and caps to be strictly first-quality goods," was not in their offer; and that, it not having been accepted as made, appellant is not bound. But it will be observed that appellant declined to furnish the goods before it got this letter, and in the correspondence with appellee it nowhere complained of these words as an addition to the contract. Quite a number of other letters passed, in which the refusal to deliver the goods was placed on other grounds, none of which have been sustained by the evidence. Appellee offers proof tending to show that these words, in the trade in which parties were engaged, conveyed the same meaning as the words used in appellant's letter, and were only a different form of expressing the same idea. Appellant's conduct would seem to confirm this evidence.

Appellant also insists that the contract was indefinite, because the quantity of each size of the jars was not fixed, that ten car loads is too indefinite a specification of the quantity sold, and that appellee had no right to accept the goods to be delivered on different days. The proof shows that "ten car loads" is an expression used in the trade as equivalent to 1,000 gross, 100 gross being regarded as a car load. The offer to sell the different sizes at different prices gave the purchaser the right to name the quantity of each size, and, the offer being to ship not later than May 15th, the buyer had the right to fix the time of delivery at any time before that. . . . The petition, if defective, was cured by the judgment, which is fully sustained by the evidence.

Judgment affirmed.

WILHELM LUBRICATION CO. v. BRATTRUD

Supreme Court of Minnesota, 1936.
197 Minn. 626, 268 N.W. 634, 106 A.L.R. 1279.

Action by the Wilhelm Lubrication Company against Wallace C. Brattrud, doing business under the name of the Economy Supply Company. From a judgment for plaintiff, defendant appeals.

Reversed and remanded.

DEVANEY, CHIEF JUSTICE. Action for damages for breach of contract for failure to accept delivery of 11,500 gallons of lubricating oil and 4,000 pounds of transmission grease.

On January 24, 1934, plaintiff and defendant entered into an agreement which reads as follows:

"The above seller hereby sells and agrees to hold in its storage for the Purchaser, and the above Purchaser hereby buys, the merchandise described below, which shall be shipped to Purchaser at Waseca, Minn., on Aug. 1st, 1934 unless ordered out sooner.

Quantity	Description	Per Gal.	Total.
5000 gals.	Worthmore Motor Oil SAE 10–70 Base	21–31	
3000 gals.	Beterlub Motor Oil SAE 10–70	26–36	
2000 gals.	Costal Motor Oil SAE 10–70	18½–28½	
1500 gals.	Penzalube Motor Oil SAE 10–70	34–44	
4000 lbs.	Black Devil Trans. Lub	5¢	
	As per Price List 34 attached	"	

[Parts of the agreement not necessary to the discussion herein are omitted.]

Approximately three weeks after the making of the above agreement, defendant repudiated the same. Plaintiff treated the contract as breached, and brought this action for damages.

The jury returned a verdict for plaintiff in the sum of $210. Defendant moved in the alternative for judgment notwithstanding or for a new trial. The motion was denied and judgment entered. This appeal is taken from the judgment.

Three questions are presented: (1) Is the agreement between the parties in whole or in part so indefinite in its terms as to be unenforceable? (2) If indefinite in part only, is the contract severable? (3) Did the court err in instructing the jury as to the measure of damages for breach of the contract?

1. In considering the first question it is necessary to explore the meaning of the terms used in the contract. Defendant, Brattrud, agreed to take a total of 11,500 gallons of oil of the different brands listed and 4,000 pounds of "Black Devil" lubricating grease. The technical term SAE 10–70 opposite each item in the contract signifies seven weights of oil officially designated by the Society of Automotive Engineers according to their thickness or viscosity. The lightest of these groups is designated SAE 10; the heaviest SAE 70; the intervening ones are, 20, 30, 40, 50, and 60. The price varies with the weight. Thus, for example, under this contract, defendant agreed to take 5,000 gallons of "Worthmore Motor Oil" of any weight he should choose from 10–70. The price for SAE 10 was 21 cents per gallon and the price for SAE 70 was 31 cents per gallon. The other weights varied in price between 21 cents and 31 cents per gallon. The same applies to the other brands of oil that defendant agreed to take.

The total quantity of each brand of oil purchased was definite. Defendant, however, had the right under the contract to specify any weight oil he wished within the weights listed. The weight controlled the price, the price of each weight being definite. But until the defendant chose a particular weight the price he was obligated to pay under the contract was not ascertained. Nor was there any agreement as to how many gallons of each weight defendant was to take. As to these matters there had been no meeting of the minds or expression of mutual assent of the parties to the contract. There was and could be no agreement as to these elements until the defendant indicated his wants within the specified limits of the alleged contract. This indefiniteness and uncertainty in the contract, is in our opinion, fatal to plaintiff's cause of action. The subject-matter of a contract of sale must be definite as to quantity and price. The reason for this requirement is obvious when we consider the question of damages. As the contract now stands with respect to the oil defendant agreed to take, the application of any measure of damages, which in case of breach of such contract must be based partly on the contract price, is impossible. Here the quantity of each brand to be taken and the contract price thereof cannot be determined until the defendant places an order. This was never done. The agreement was repudiated before any order was placed. The court or jury cannot be allowed to speculate as to the measure of damages, and there is no sound authority for taking an average or an arbitrary price as the contract price in a case of this kind. This, in effect, would be inserting a new term in the contract, thereby remaking the agreement for the parties, which is beyond the power of a court or jury.

In the case of Wheeling Steel & Iron Co. v. Evans, 97 Md. 305, 55 A. 373, a contract of sale involving the same problem as the one in this case was before the court. The buyer had agreed to take 100 tons of tack plate. There were four grades, two at one price and two at another. It was held that no enforceable contract was created as there was no agreement as to how much of each grade the purchaser was to take, and the purchase price could not be ascertained until the purchaser designated which he wanted. The court said: "If the purchaser had the option to specify for any or all of the four gauges, it is clear that, until such specifications had been made, there could be no definite agreement, because it was the purchaser's privilege and right to designate 100 tons of No. 12, or of No. 14, or of No. 15, or of No. 16, or 25 tons of each gauge, or any other of a vast multitude of different proportions of the whole four gauges, or of any two or three of them. The price of each gauge was definite; the total quantity of tons was definite, and the times of delivery were definite; but the proportion of each gauge, as well as which of the four would be required, is wholly indefinite and uncertain. As to that element of the alleged contract there was obviously no consensus ad idem. . . . The test . . . lies in considering what would have been the measure of damages in a suit instituted by the vendor against the vendee for a breach of the alleged contract. Would the vendor have been entitled to recover the difference between the contract price and the market price of the whole 100 tons, reckoned on the basis of $2.80 per 100 pounds, or on the basis of $2.72 per 100 pounds, or on some other basis founded on an arbitrary apportionment of the whole number of tons amongst the four different gauges? . . . What quantity of each gauge could a court or jury declare that the vendee ought to have specified? If either court or jury had undertaken such a task, it would have supplied a term of the contract which the parties themselves failed to incorporate, and manifestly such a proceeding would have been unwarranted." [Cases cited.]

The compelling logic of the foregoing line of decisions, coupled with the obvious fact that the adoption of any other rule would result in innumerable difficulties and cause much confusion in actual operation, leads us to the conclusion that in an agreement of this kind, the subject-matter of the contract is too indefinite to be capable of identification, and no action will lie for breach thereof. . . .

As to the portion of the agreement which provides for defendant's purchase of 4,000 pounds of lubricating grease, the contract is clearly not indefinite. The brand, "Black Devil" is definite. The quantity, 4,000 pounds, and the price, 5 cents per pound, are likewise certain and definite. There is no discretion allowed the buyer, defendant, in either amount or price. Plaintiff is entitled to recover damages for breach of this part of the agreement if the agreement is legally severable. . . . [The court's discussion of question (2) is omitted.]

We conclude that the contract is severable and that plaintiff is entitled to recover damages for breach of this portion of the agreement. . . . [The court's discussion of question (3) is omitted.]

Because part of the contract in this case is unenforceable, and the question of damages was submitted to the jury with reference to the whole thereof, the decision of the court below must be reversed, and the case remanded for a new trial on the question of damages only in accordance with the views herein set forth.

So ordered.

WILLMOTT v. GIARRAPUTO, 5 N.Y.2d 250, 184 N.Y.S.2d 97, 157 N.E.2d 282 (1959). [Giarraputo gave the Willmotts a six month option to buy property. The option agreement described the property, the price, and the amount of the purchase-money mortgage; but provided with respect to that mortgage that "the payment of interest and amortization of principal shall be mutually agreed upon at the time of entering into a more formal contract." When the Willmotts elected to exercise the option, Giarraputo's lawyer submitted a contract to them, which they declined to sign because it did not contain a prepayment term. Their lawyer then modified the contract by inserting a pre-payment term, and they signed and returned it to Giarraputo, who refused to sign the modified contract. The Willmotts then instituted an action for specific performance. They appeal from a dismissal of their complaint.]

FULD, J. . . . Few principles are better settled in the law of contract than the proposition that, if a material element of a contemplated contract is left for future negotiations, there is no contract. . . ." Here . . . the option agreement expressly recites that the "payment of interest and amortization of principal" provided for in the mortgage were to be "mutually agreed upon at the time of entering into a more formal contract." And, as one of the plaintiffs actually testified, the parties never agreed upon that matter. Not only were the plaintiffs dissatisfied with the contract drafted by the defendant's lawyer, but their own attorney made a still further amendment to the contract, with respect to prepayment, which the parties had, so far as appears, never even discussed.

[Affirmed.]

DOHRMAN v. SULLIVAN

Court of Appeals of Kentucky, 1949.
310 Ky. 463, 220 S.W.2d 973.

[Suit by Howard A. Sullivan and another against Heer Dohrman and another for specific performance of a contract to convey realty. From an adverse judgment defendants appeal. Judgment affirmed.]

STANLEY, COMMISSIONER. The judgment directs specific performance of a contract to convey real estate.

The question is whether there was a completed contract or merely negotiations in contemplation by both parties to enter into a formal contract which was never in fact executed.

The appellants, Heer Dohrman and Charlotte Dohrman, owners of residence property in Covington, had placed it in the hands of a Cincinnati real estate broker for sale under a written contract which expired, after extension, on March 5, 1946. But the agent kept the key to the house and continued its sign on the premises. Through a Covington real estate agent, Howard F. Sullivan and his wife procured the key, examined the property, and on March 29 executed a written offer to buy the property. It was addressed to the Cincinnati agent, a corporation, which sent a telegram to the owners, who were in Florida, advising them it had sold the property to the Sullivans for $10,250 cash and asked confirmation and for certain information for preparation of the deed. On the same day the owners by mail acknowledged the telegram, congratulated the brokers on obtaining a purchaser, expressed the hope that all arrangements would be completed and the sale effected. They gave definite information about the size of the lot and the title and stated they would see that the broker had all information should the sale go through. There was an exchange of several letters regarding taxes, expenses, etc. All of these things were eventually agreed upon. Of particular importance is this statement in Dohrman's letter of April 10: "If the answers are to our satisfaction, we will immediately forward the sales contract which we have prepared which contains the terms of the agreement. This of course would act as a confirmation of the sale. If a sale is confirmed, I shall forward the deed. I have decided

to draft it myself." Finally, on April 17 Dohrman
wrote the agent enclosing three copies of a formal sales
contract for the "prospective purchasers" to sign. This
instrument stated that Heer Dohrman and Charlotte
Dohrman had "bargained and sold" the described property to Howard F. and Agnes Sullivan for the agreed
price of $10,250 to be paid in cash and also the agree-
ment as to the taxes and time of possession. In this letter Dohrman requested that when the Sullivans had
signed the acceptance, which he had written on the instrument, "we will sign them, retain one for ourselves
and return to you a copy for them and a copy for your
company's record." The acceptance provision of the
sales contract was promptly signed by the Sullivans
and returned to Dohrman in Florida on April 19 by the
agent. In its letter transmitting the acceptance reference was made to the examination of the title by an attorney and that he had called attention to the absence
of a record of payment of inheritance taxes on the
estate of Dohrman's mother from whom he had inherited the property. The question is whether this letter
and the acceptance by the Sullivans constituted a complete and binding contract, for the Dohrmans never
did sign the formal sales contract or return any copy
of it to the agent or to the Sullivans. Dohrman merely
advised his agent that when the matter of inheritance
taxes had been investigated he would communicate further with him. To this the agent replied that the purchaser's attorney had advised it would be agreeable to
close the transaction at once, paying over the net proceeds less $300, which could be put in escrow until the
inheritance tax question should be settled. A few days
later the agent telegraphed Dohrman that the purchaser was complaining about the delay in closing the

deal and asked about his intention to do so. Dohrman replied that he did not agree to withholding $300 and that he did not intend to convey the property until his title or right to do so was completely vested in himself and that he did not care to be worried unduly about the transaction. Finally, on May 10 Dohrman wrote his agent that circumstances had arisen which prevented him disposing of his house and that he intended to return to Covington and occupy it.

The Chancellor was of opinion that the defendants' letter of April 17, above described, with which was enclosed the formal sales contract was a sufficient memorandum under the statute of frauds to bind them through the written acceptance of the other parties; that this constituted an offer to sell and an unconditional acceptance. The court pointed to portions of the defendants' previous letters of April 10 and 17, above quoted, with the return to them on the 19th of the signed contract as sufficient to bind them. We think this was the proper construction of the transaction. There was no condition attached, and it was not necessary that they should have in addition signed their own proposal to sell the property after it had been accepted and have transmitted a copy of that signed proposal to the purchaser.

Preliminary negotiations leading up to the execution of a contract are distinguishable from the contract itself; likewise, a mere agreement to reach an agreement, which imposes no obligation on the parties thereto. It is sometimes a close question whether correspondence between parties constitutes final and complete mutual assent or meeting of minds, essential to the creation of a contract. The correspondence may constitute only negotiation and but evidence their intention ultimately to form or to execute a contract. The question of whether there was a consummated contract is to be determined from the consideration and practical construction of all the separate letters or telegrams that make up the whole correspondence. . . .

The Restatement of the Law of Contracts, Vol. 1, sec. 26, thus states the applicable rule: "Mutual manifestations of assent that are in themselves sufficient to make a contract will not be prevented from so operating by the mere fact that the parties also manifest an intention to prepare and adopt a written memorial thereof; but other facts may show that the manifestations are merely preliminary expressions." To state the rule less abstractly: Where all the substantial terms of a contract have been agreed on and there is nothing left for future settlement, the fact alone that the parties contemplated execution of a formal instrument as a convenient memorial or definitive record of the agreement does not leave the transaction incomplete and without binding force in the absence of a positive agreement that it should not be binding until so executed. 12 Am.Jur., Contracts, secs. 23, 25.

In our early case of Bell v. Offutt, 10 Bush 632, 73 Ky. 632, the court said: "If two persons enter into a verbal agreement about a matter as to which an enforceable parol contract can be made, it would be no defense, when one of them is sued for a breach of the contract, that he understood it would not be obligatory unless reduced to writing; nor does a contemporaneous agreement to reduce a contract to writing make its validity depend upon its being actually reduced to writing and signed. The agreement to put it in writing amounts to no more than an agreement by the parties to provide a particular kind of evidence of the terms of their contract, and no more prevents its enforcement upon other legal evidence than an agreement that they would go to a named individual and state to him the terms of their contract would render the testimony of any other competent witness inadmissible to prove what the contract was." . . .

If all the material terms which are to be incorporated into the contemplated future instrument have been agreed upon, it may be inferred that the instrument is to be a mere memorial of the contract already final by the earlier mutual assent of the parties to those terms. Rosenfield v. United States Trust Co., 290 Mass. 210, 195 N.E. 323, 122 A.L.R. 1210. In the instant case, all the terms and conditions had been agreed to as shown by the telegrams and letters exchanged between the Dohrmans and their agent and its transactions with the purchasers in connection therewith. This is manifested by the fact that the vendors of the property had prepared the "sales contract" and sent it through their agent to the vendees who accepted the instrument. The matter of putting $300 in escrow had been merely proposed and was never made a condition to buying the property. The vendors' offer had already been accepted. It is true that the owners had not then signed the paper and only contemplated doing so after the acceptance form had been signed by the vendees. They are bound, nevertheless, by their signature to the letter which transmitted it since there was a delivery back to them of the acceptance of what was under the circumstances a definite proposal to sell their property. . . . In the instant case we have a very definite and complete acceptance and delivery to the sellers of their written proposal. Thus there was a completed instrument, mutually binding upon the parties. We are of opinion, therefore, that the judgment is correct.

Judgment affirmed.

STEINMEYER v. *SCHROEPPEL*

CARTWRIGHT, J. Appellants are in the lumber business at Collinsville, Ill., and appellee is a building contractor at the same place. On June 10, 1905, appellee was about to erect a building for himself, and left at the office of appellants an itemized list of lumber, containing 34 items, on which he desired them to give him a price. Appellants' bookkeeper set down upon that list, opposite each item, the selling price, but did not add up the column. If correctly added, the column would have footed up $1,867. One of the appellants made the addition, and, by mistake, made the total $1,446. The bookkeeper copied the list on one of appellants' billheads without the prices opposite the different items, and wrote at the bottom, "Above for $1,446," and delivered the paper to appellee the same evening. Appellee received bids for the lumber from two other firms, which were in the neighborhood of $1,890. On June 16th appellee called at the office of appellants and accepted their offer. He did not bring the paper with him, but the bookkeeper made another copy and at the bottom of it wrote the same memorandum, "Above for $1,446." One of the appellants signed it, and a memorandum was then written below to the effect that if delivery was made within 30 days the appellants were to have $20 more than the estimate, but if delivery was made after 30 days appellee was to have a rebate of $20 from the estimate, and this was signed by both parties.

The same evening one of the appellants, looking over
the bill, found that he had not added the amounts correctly, and the next morning one of them notified appellee by telephone of the mistake, and refused to furnish the lumber for less than $1,867. Appellants also
sent appellee a notice that they had found an error of
$421, and the estimate should read $1,867 instead of
$1,446. Appellants did not furnish the lumber, and ap-
pellee purchased it at the next lowest bid from another
firm, and sued appellants for the difference between
what he paid for the lumber, and what they had agreed
to furnish it for. Appellants then filed a bill to enjoin
the prosecution of the suit at law, and to have the contract canceled on account of the mistake. The suits were
consolidated and tried together without a jury. The circuit court entered a decree canceling the contract, and
restraining appellee from prosecuting his suit at law.
The Appellate Court for the Fourth District reversed
the decree, and remanded the cause to the circuit court,
with directions to dissolve the injunction and dismiss
the bill for want of equity. Appellants applied to the
Appellate Court for a certificate of importance, which
was granted, and this appeal was prosecuted.

The jurisdiction of equity to grant the remedy of
cancellation because of a mistake of fact by one party
to a contract is well recognized. Mutual consent is
requisite to the creation of a contract, and if there is
a mistake of fact by one of the parties going to the
essence of the contract, no agreement is, in fact, made.
2 Kent's Com. 477. If there is apparently a valid contract in writing, but by reason of a mistake of fact by
one of the parties, not due to his negligence, the contract is different with respect to the subject-matter
or terms from what was intended, equity will give to

such party a remedy by cancellation where the parties can be placed in statu quo. The ground for relief is, that by reason of the mistake there was no mutual assent to the terms of the contract. 24 Am. & Eng.Ency. of Law (2d Ed.) 618. The fact concerning which the mistake was made must be material to the transaction and affect its substance, and the mistake must not result from want of the care and diligence exercised by persons of reasonable prudence under the same circumstances. Bonney v. Stoughton; 122 Ill. 536, 13 N.E. 833. In this case the mistake was in the addition of the figures set down by the bookkeeper. The price of each item was written correctly, but appellants claimed that one item of about $400 was placed somewhat to the right, and in adding the column the 4 was counted in the 10-column instead of the 100-column. If that was done, it does not account for the difference of $421. But if it did, it would only show a want of ordinary care and attention. If the figures were not exactly in line, the fact could hardly escape notice by a competent business man giving reasonable attention to what he was doing. There was no evidence tending to prove any special circumstances excusing the blunder.

The case of Board of School Com'rs v. Bender, 36 Ind.App. 164, 72 N.E. 154 (decided by the Appellate Court of Indiana, Division No. 2) relied on by appellants, differs from this in various respects, one of which is that Bender was excusable for the mistake. His complaint alleged that he was misinformed by the architect that his bid must be in at or before 4 o'clock, when, in fact, he was allowed until 8 o'clock; that in ignorance of the fact and for want of time he was hurried in submitting his bid, and had no opportunity for verification of his estimate, and that under those circumstances he turned two leaves of his estimate book by mistake and omitted an estimate on a large part of the work. The case involved the question whether the bidder had forfeited a sum deposited as a guaranty that he would enter into a contract, and when notified that his bid was accepted, having discovered his mistake, he informed the architect and immediately gave notice that he would not enter into the contract. By the terms of the bid it was intended that if the bid was accepted a contract would be made, but the bid was not the contract contemplated by the parties and the bidder never did enter into the contract. The court concluded that the minds of the parties never, in fact, met, because the bidder fell into the error without his fault. In the case of Harran v. Foley, 62 Wis. 584, 22 N.W. 837, there was no agreement, for the reason that the minds of the parties never met. The plaintiff claimed to have purchased of the defendant some cattle for $161.50, but the defendant intended to state the price at $261.50. When the defendant was informed that the plaintiff understood the price to be $161.50 he refused to deliver the cattle and tendered back $20 received on the purchase price. No agreement was, in fact, made, since the statement of the price by the seller was clearly a mistake.

A mistake which will justify relief in equity must affect the substance of the contract, and not a mere incident or the inducement for entering into it. The mistake of the appellants did not relate to the subject-matter of the contract, its location, identity, or amount, and there was neither belief in the existence of a fact which did not exist or ignorance of any fact material to the contract which did exist. The contract was exactly what each party understood it to be and it expressed what was intended by each. If it can be set aside on account of the error in adding up the amounts representing the selling price, it could be set aside for a mistake in computing the percentage of profits which appellants intended to make, or on account of a mistake in the cost of the lumber to them, or any other miscalculation on their part. If equity would relieve on account of such a mistake there would be no stability in contracts, and we think the Appellate Court was right in concluding that the mistake was not of such a character as to entitle the appellants to the relief prayed for.

The judgment of the Appellate Court is affirmed. Judgment affirmed.

GEREMIA v. BOYARSKY

Supreme Court of Errors of Connecticut, 1928
107 Conn. 387, 140 A. 749.

[Action to recover damages for breach of building contract by Sylvester Geremia against Morris Boyarsky and others. Judgment for defendant, and plaintiff appeals. No error.]

BANKS, J. The defendants are carpenters and building contractors, and in April, 1926, the plaintiff requested them to submit bids for the carpenter work and painting for a house that he was building for himself. The defendants met in the evening of April 25th for the purpose of making their estimates, but did not complete their figures, owing to the lateness of the hour. They wrote their estimates on two separate pieces of paper, but did not add the figures. The next morning the plaintiff called upon the defendants, and requested the defendant Boyarsky to stop the work that he was upon and complete the estimate. Boyarsky sat down with the plaintiff at a workbench, and proceeded to add up the various items upon the two sheets. In his haste, he made an error in adding the items on the first sheet, footing them up at $99.10, when the correct footing should have been $859.10. This error, being carried to the second sheet, made the apparent cost of the work $1,450.00, instead of $2,210.40. The plaintiff thereupon awarded the contract to the defendants, and later the same day they executed a written contract to do the work for the sum of $1,450.40. The plaintiff, when the erroneous bid was given, and when he procured the signing of the contract, had good reason to believe and know that there must have been a substantial omission or error in the amount of the bid. That evening the defendants discovered their mistake, and, as soon as they could find the plaintiff, notified him of the mistake, and offered to go forward with the work according to the actual prices carried out in their estimate, and as low as any responsible contractor would do it for, if less than $2,210.40. The plaintiff refused their offer, and insisted that they complete the work for $1,450.40. The sum of $2,375 was a reasonable price for the work covered by the defendants' contract, and the plaintiff thereafter let the contract for the work to other contractors for that sum. The court found that the defendants had made a material mistake in their bid, that it would be inequitable to award the plaintiff damages for a breach of the contract, and that it should be rescinded.

The finding is not subject to correction in any material respect. In paragraph 12 the item $959.10 should be $859.10, and is corrected accordingly.

The finding discloses a case where the defendants,

by reason of an error in computation, have obligated themselves to perform a contract for a sum substantially less than the sum which the actual figures of their estimate totaled, and less than the reasonable cost of the work contracted to be done. It is the contention of the plaintiff that equity should not relieve the defendants from the consequences of their mistake, because (a) it was a unilateral mistake; (b) it was not material to the making of the contract; and (c) it resulted from the defendants' own negligence. While the mistake of only one of the parties inducing him to sign a contract cannot be a ground for a reformation of the contract, it may be a ground for its cancellation. Snelling v. Merritt, 85 Conn. 83, 101, 81 A. 1039. Though the mistake was not induced by the conduct of the other party, equity will grant relief, if the latter, when he becomes aware of the mistake, seeks to take an unconscionable advantage of it. Lieberum v. Nussenbaum, 94 Conn. 276, 108 A. 662. The plaintiff, though he is found by the court not to have participated in the mistake, had good reason to believe that one had been made before the contract was signed, was notified of the mistake by the defendants before he had changed his position in any respect, and sought to take unfair advantage of it by insisting upon the performance of the contract at a price upon which the minds of the parties had never met. When the contract is still executory and the parties can be put in statu quo, one party to the contract will not be permitted to obtain an unconscionable advantage merely because the mistake was unilateral. 3 Williston on Contracts, §§ 1578, 1580.

That a mistake through which the defendants agreed to perform the contract for a price one-third less than the total of the actual figures of their estimate was of so essential and fundamental a character that the minds of the parties never met would not seem to require discussion.

As a general rule, a party will not be given relief against a mistake induced by his own culpable negligence. "But the rule is not inflexible, and in many cases relief may be granted although the mistake was not unmixed with some element of negligence, particularly where the other party has been in no way prejudiced." Fountain Co. v. Stein, 97 Conn. 619, 626, 118 A. 47, 49 (27 A.L.R. 976); Petterson v. Weinstock, 106 Conn. 436, 445, 138 A. 433, 437; 21 Corpus Juris, 88. "The conclusion from the best authorities seems to be that the neglect must amount to a violation of a positive legal duty. The highest possible care is not demanded. Even a clearly established negligence may not of itself be a sufficient ground for refusing relief if it appears that the other party was not prejudiced thereby." 2 Pomeroy's Eq.Juris. (4th Ed.) § 856. "If one of the parties through mistake names a consideration that is out of all proportion to the value of the subject of negotiations, and the other party, realizing that a mistake must have been made, takes advantage of it, and refuses to let the mistake be corrected when it is discovered, he cannot under these conditions claim an enforceable contract." 6 R.C.L. 623.

It may be conceded that the error in addition made by the defendant Boyarsky, when he hastily totaled the items of his estimate at the request of the plaintiff, involved some degree of negligence. It would be inequitable under the circumstances to permit the plaintiff, who had good reason to know, before the contract was signed, that there must have been a substantial omission or error in the amount of the bid, to take advantage of such error while the contract was still executory, and he had been in no way prejudiced, and to require the defendants to do the work for an amount much less than the actual cost. In similar situations when a price has been bid which, because of erroneous arithmetical processes, or by the omission of items, was based on a mistake, rescission has been allowed where the contract was still executory, and it would be inequitable to permit the other party to gain an unfair advantage from a mistake which has not prejudiced him in any way. . . .

The mistake of the defendants was of so fundamental a character that the minds of the parties did not meet. It was not, under the circumstances, the result of such culpable negligence as to bar the defendants of redress, and the plaintiff, before the contract was signed, had good reason to believe that a substantial error had been made, and, while the contract was still executory, and he had been in no way prejudiced, refused to permit the correction of the error, and attempted to take an unconscionable advantage of it. The defendants were clearly entitled to a decree canceling the contract.

There is no error.

All concur.

Briefs of the foregoing cases would produce statements such as the following:

BALFOUR v. BALFOUR

H (Holding)—Agreements (husband and wife) which the parties do *not* intend to have legal consequences are not enforceable.

R (Rationale)—(1) Actual intent of parties. (2) Impractical (torrent of litigation).

CRAFT v. ELDER

H—The typical advertisement or published pricelist is not an offer, but only an invitation to negotiate.

R—Restatement of Contracts, and other treatises.

LEFKOWITZ v. GREAT MINNEAPOLIS SURPLUS STORE

H—An advertisement which leaves nothing open for negotiation is an offer (Dictum—whether an advertisement is an offer depends upon the parties' legal intentions and the surrounding circumstances).

OWEN v. TUNISON

H—The words "I couldn't sell unless I was to receive X amount" constitute an invitation, not an offer (even though in response to offer to buy in specific amount).

HARVEY v. FACEY

H—Statement of lowest price (in response to words, "will you sell X, what is lowest price) does not constitute offer to sell X.

FAIRMOUNT GLASS WORKS v. CRUNDEN-MARTIN WOODENWARE CO.

H—Response to request to "state terms" which includes words "for immediate acceptance" constitutes an offer (even though response also included words "we quote you").

R—Intention of the parties.

WILHELM LUBRICATING CO. v. *BRATTRUD*

H—An offer which permits the offeree to select the quantity and quality of goods (and thereby the price) is too indefinite. (Selection had not been made.)

H—A finite portion of a contract is severable from that which is not.

R—(1) Impracticability of determining damages, and (2) subject matter of contract must be definite as to quantity and price.

WILLMOTT v. *GIARRAPUTO*

H—No contract exists where a material element (payment of interest and amortization of principal) remains for future negotiations.

R—Must be agreement on key terms.

DOHRMAN v. *SULLIVAN*

H—Lack of a party's signature to a writing will not prevent formation of a contract where agreement on material terms, unless agreement to that effect. (Party who failed to sign had indicated in a letter that he would execute agreement.)

STEINMEYER v. *SCHROEPPEL*

H—Unilateral mistake due to lack of care (computation error) is not grounds for voiding a contract (even though offeree informed immediately). (Dictum—if mistake of fact, may be different result.)

GEREMIA v. *BOYARSKY*

H—Unilateral mistake will avoid contract where other side (1) had reason to believe mistake had been made, and/or (2) had not changed its position. (Dictum—one party cannot take unconscionable advantage of the mistake of another.)

R—No meeting of the minds.

You have not assembled all of the relevant materials until classnotes and the pertinent legislation, if any, have also been examined. Several provisions of the Uniform Commercial Code (abbreviated UCC) relate to the problem of what constitutes an enforceable offer or acceptance: Section 2-102 states, "Unless the context otherwise requires, this Article applies to transactions in goods"; "Goods" are defined in § 2-105(1) to mean, *inter alia*: ". . . all things (including specially manufactured goods) which are moveable. . . ." Section 2-204(3) declares: "Even though one or more terms are left open, a contract for sale does not fail for indefiniteness if the parties have intended to make a contract and there is a reasonably certain basis for giving an appropriate remedy." Finally, § 2-305 provides, *inter alia*: "(1) the parties, if they so intend, can conclude a contract for sale even though the price is not settled. In such a case the price is a reasonable price at the time of delivery if (a) nothing is said as to price; or (b) the price is left to be agreed upon by the parties and they fail to agree; . . . (2) a price to be fixed by the seller or by the buyer means a price for him to fix in good faith. . . . (4) Where, however, the parties intend not to be bound unless the price is fixed or agreed and it is not fixed or agreed, there is no contract."

A synthesis of the above briefs and legislation could be the following:

An Enforceable Offer Exists Where

(1) *It is not an invitation:*

(a) "I couldn't sell unless I was to receive X amount" is an invitation (*Owen* v. *Tunison*); and bald statement of lowest price in response to request is an invitation, *Harvey* v. *Facey.*

(b) "For immediate acceptance" in response to request to "state terms" is an offer (even though response included words "We quote you"). *Fairmount* v. *Crunden.*

(c) Typical newspaper advertisement is an invitation, *Craft* v. *Elder,* except where nothing is left open for negotiation, *Lefkowitz* v. *Great Minn.* (Dictum— Intention of parties will govern.)

AND

(2) *It is definite as to:*

(a) *Quantity* and *price* of each item (*Wilhelm* v. *Brattrud*), (but a finite portion of a contract may be severed.) R—Impracticability of determining damages, *and all.*

(b) *Material terms* (i.e., interest rate and amortization of principal) *Willmott* v. *Giarraputo.*

BUT

UCC § 2-204(3) states that a contract may exist even though open terms if (i) *intention to contract,* and (ii) *reasonably certain basis* for giving appropriate remedy, and *under UCC § 2-305* a reasonable price will be fixed by the court if (i) nothing said, (ii) parties fail to agree upon a term left open for subsequent *agreement,* or (iii) price to be fixed by one of parties—but, price will *not* be fixed where parties have agreed that no contract will be created unless they agree upon a price, and they do not. Thus, UCC (which applies to sale of goods) liberalizes rules pertaining to the formation of a contract.

AND

(3) Even though a writing is not executed by the parties. (*Dohrman* v. *Sullivan*).

EXCEPT WHERE

(1) Neither party intends their agreement to have legal consequences (*Balfour* v. *Balfour*) R—actual intent, torrent of litigation, *OR*

(2) The offeror can't comprehend legal consequences of acts (*Lucy* v. *Zehmer*), *OR*

(3) A contract is not intended, and other party knows it; *otherwise* each party deemed to have intention equivalent to words and/or acts (*Lucy* v. *Zehmer*).

(4) Mistake in computation made, *and* other party has reason to know it (and/or has not changed its position? but this may be dictum) *Geremia* v. *Boyarsky*; otherwise unilateral mistake due to lack of care is not grounds for avoidance, *Steinmeyer* v. *Schroeppel* (even though no change in position).

An explanation of why the synthesized cases were arranged as set forth above is now in order. The first case, *Balfour* v. *Balfour*, stands for the proposition that certain types of agreements are not attended by legal consequences, even though there has been an ostensible offer and acceptance. This decision is not really concerned with the validity of a particular offer, but rather, represents an example of a type of agreement which is not enforceable. It is thus an *exception t*o the general rule that where a valid offer is accepted a contract results.

In a similar vein, *Lucy* v. *Zehmer* did not deal with the requisites of a bona fide offer. Instead, this opinion demonstrates the proposition that a party will be bound by his overt actions (be they words or deeds), regardless of any secret intent, unless the other side was somehow aware of the unexpressed intention. Thus, *Lucy* v. *Zehmer* is concerned primarily with the fact that legal consequences will attach to one's outward manifestations.

Craft v. *Elder* and *Lefkowitz* v. *Great Minneapolis* opened up the more substantive "invitation/offer" problem, but these decisions are confined to a relatively narrow area —the newspaper advertisement. *Owen* v. *Tunison, Harvey* v. *Facey* and *Fairmount* v. *Crunden* are illustrative of the broader aspects of this problem. These cases indicate that communications among the parties must be analyzed to determine whether a given party's words and/or conduct have given rise to an offer which creates an enforceable obligation when accepted.

Wilhelm v. *Brattrud* and *Willmott* v. *Giarraputo* deal with a different type of controversy; the completeness or definiteness of an offer. The former decision indicated that even if a legitimate offer is intended, and accepted, either side is free to withdraw with legal impunity, at least until the quantity and price of each item is determined. However, the holding of *Wilhelm* v. *Brattrud* may have been undercut by the UCC provisions applicable to this question. Oil is certainly a "good" so the UCC would govern this type of transaction. Of course, if the property being sold was not a "good," it could still be contended that the UCC provisions cited above embody a legislative policy to enforce contracts even though some terms are not explicitly agreed upon. Sections 2-204 and 2-305 of the UCC indicate that an enforceable contract can be created even though the price has been omitted. A party attempting to avoid a contract would still be able to argue that other material terms (i.e., the terms, place and time of payment) had not been resolved and therefore no contract had been created, citing *Willmott* v. *Giarraputo*.

Dohrman v. *Sullivan* deals primarily with a different problem, where there is accord on the essential terms, but the agreement has not been reduced to a writing (or the writing has not been signed). *Steinmeyer* v. *Schroeppel* and *Geremia* v. *Boyarsky* are concerned with the unilateral mistake problem. The question mark within the holding of the latter case in the synthesis indicates the opinion is not clear as to whether either of the two situations (reason to know and change of position) will avoid a mistake, or both must be present. If the latter ground was determinative, *Geremia* v. *Boyarsky* would be in conflict with the *Steinmeyer* case, where a binding contract was found to exist even though the offeree was notified of the error the very next day and apparently had not changed his position.

As noted in the initial paragraph of this chapter, the key to organizing synthesized materials is arranging them in the sequence in which they would be most likely to happen if a situation could be conceived which brought every possible legal principle into play. This can be accomplished only if you understand how the various propositions of law are interrelated. A threshold inquiry in determining if a valid offer was made would be "Was the communication which one party seeks to characterize as an offer, merely an invitation?" If the latter were true, no agreement would arise from its acceptance. However, if a "true" offer had been made, the next logical focus would be upon the terms, "Were they legally sufficient?" If the foregoing hurdles were overcome, the next question might be whether the fact that one of the parties believed that a signed writing was necessary to imbue the agreement with legal consequences is a sufficient ground to nullify the transaction?

Assuming a valid offer was made, the next potential problem area would be, "Are there any grounds for refusing to enforce it, nevertheless?" The fact that one of the parties was only joking will not relieve such party of his contractual obligations unless the other actually knew said party was not serious. Neither will a unilateral mistake resulting from carelessness (unless the other party had reason to know that an error had ·been made) usually justify avoidance of one's agreements, although no change of position by the offeree prior to notification *may* be grounds for a contrary outcome. Intoxication may be a defense, although the reference to this point was dictum. A final problem could be, "Whether the transaction is one of those rare instances in which the law will presume no legally enforceable contract was intended despite an ostensible offer and acceptance?" (*Balfour* v. *Balfour*).

It should be emphasized that the synthesis set forth above is not the only *correct* or *right* one. Any synthesis of the foregoing subchapter would be an effective study tool, provided that it (1) highlights the *main* problem areas represented by the synthesized cases, and (2) is arranged, as nearly as possible, in the order or sequence in which the issues inherent in each principle would be considered in a factual situation which contained all of them, and (3) is no longer than absolutely necessary. Organizing course materials in such a manner requires time and thought. However, it is time well spent since synthesizing develops your ability to "tie the course together" (i.e. recognize the interrelationship of the materials).

Several general observations can be made from the sample synthesis set forth above. First, the amorphous mass of materials in the subchapter has been distilled into the basic propositions of law which were contained therein. By reducing twenty-four pages of text into a few distinguishable potential problem areas and about 40 lines, the likelihood of recalling the issues which might be contained in a hypothetical involving an "offer" question is greatly enhanced. Consideration of the prospective issues should occur in an orderly, systematic manner. Next, the truly important (i.e., that which would probably be useful for test purposes) facts and dictum have been inserted into the niche at which a discussion of them would be likely to occur. Finally, case names are inserted immediately after the principle which they represent. It should be mentioned, however, that memorization of case names is usually not expected by the grader.

Once it is completed, each mini-synthesis should be analyzed for the purpose of anticipating words or phrases which would be likely sources of issues on a final exam. Applying this suggestion to the synthesis of the subchapter pertaining to "Offer," an analysis would proceed as follows: (1) approximately four cases dealt with the "offer/invitation" problem; also, it is the type of issue which can usually be argued both ways (i.e. each party can point to some statement or acts by the other which would justifiably lead one to believe that an agreement has, or has not, been reached); therefore, this problem is a good candidate to appear on an exam, (2) the "definiteness" problem is also likely to be found on the finals; not only were two cases concerned with this issue, but so were each of the UCC provisions (which are directly applicable if "goods" are involved); also, words and phrases in rules of law such as "if the parties have *intended* to make a contract" and "*reasonably* certain basis" (contained in UCC Section 2-204) are highly relative in nature and therefore invite debate. Whether or not one of the parties believed a writing, or his signature thereon, was a prerequisite to a valid offer; and whether any of the issues inherent in any of the exceptions to an otherwise enforceable offer are present, should be fairly obvious.

Consideration of Completed Syntheses

Step 3 is to imagine hypothetical situations which explore the parameters of the synthesized materials. For example, Mr. A sends out a flyer to his regular customers, including Mr. B, which states that as a result of improved production processes, "all this week I will be selling red marbles at 10¢ off, and blue marbles at 20¢ off." Upon receipt of the letter, B immediately sends A a telegram which states, "Send me 400 marbles as per your flyer." B meant to order 200 marbles of each color, but in his haste to take advantage of the lower prices, neglected to specify the amount of each type. Two days later, B receives a telegram from A stating that, "Due to mechanical failures, cannot accept your order." Could B successfully contend that A's offer was enforceable and therefore A is liable to B?

Obviously, A would argue that the prices described in his mailing to B were simply quotations, and the flyer merely invited B to make an offer to purchase at those prices. A could cite *Craft* v. *Elder* in support of his contention. However, B could argue in rebuttal that because (1) the mailing was sent to a limited group of persons, rather than to the public at large, and (2) the flyer stated "I will be selling" specific goods for a definite period of time, these factors taken together prove A's mailing constituted an offer. B could cite *Fairmount* v. *Crunden* and *Lefkowitz* v. *Great Minnesota* as decisions which tend to support his position.

A would also argue that even if his mailing could be deemed an offer, no contract could have arisen anyway since not only is the quantity of each type of marble unresolved by B's telegram, but also, nothing specific has been said as to the cost thereof. This situation is even more vague than that described in *Wilhelm* v. *Brattrud,* where at least the goods had minimum and maximum prices. There is absolutely no basis upon which damages could be determined, since the price and number of each color marble is unknown. Finally, A would assert that other material elements are missing: Responsibility for delivery of the marbles (will A ship them or will B pick them up at A's premises), how quickly delivery be made, who will pay the cost of shipment, would payment be C.O.D. or over a period of time?

Although A's arguments are ostensibly persuasive, B could respond along the following lines: Marbles are within the definition of "goods," and since this transaction is governed by the UCC any prior inconsistent case law has been superseded; § 2-305 of the UCC states that where cost is not mentioned a "reasonable price" will be fixed by the court; if we assume that red marbles had been selling for $.30 and blue marbles for $.40, a reasonable price for the red and blue ones would be $.20 each; § 2-204(3) of the UCC states that where an agreement was intended an enforceable contract exists if there is a "reasonably appropriate" basis for awarding damages; that an agreement was intended is supported by the fact that A's flyer stated that "I will be selling," and A did not cancel his offer because it was only meant to be an invitation or because B's response was too indefinite, but rather, A expressly stated that "mechanical problems" were the cause of cancellation; B could also state that his words "400 red and blue marbles" would reasonably be construed to mean 200 of each, and if A was truely puzzled by B's response, why didn't he request clarification; next, B would contend that a "reasonably appropriate" basis for awarding damages would be to charge A with failing to make delivery of 400 of either the red or blue marbles; finally, the place and terms of delivery are not "material terms," and besides, A reneged on his offer before B could supply the details of these ancillary aspects of the transaction. Certainly, B would argue, his proposed remedy is preferable to permitting A to avoid his obligation completely.

The foregoing analysis to the hypothetical posed above constitutes an example of what is meant by *discussing* an issue. On an exam, after an issue is defined, you will be expected to set forth every argument which each side to the controversy would assert to persuade the court (or a jury) to resolve each issue in its favor. In responding to a legal problem, it is important for you to remember to play the devil's advocate (i.e. exert the same amount of enthusiasm and diligence for each side). While the equities of a particular hypothetical situation may lead you to be sympathetic to one of the parties, failure to set forth complete arguments will probably be construed by the grader as ignorance of the omitted points (and your mark will suffer correspondingly).

Consideration of hypothetical situations such as that described above are tremendously important. It sharpens your understanding of the applicability of the synthesized materials to new circumstances, and thereby increases the likelihood that you will recognize such material when it appears in less obvious form on the final. They also develop your capacity to make arguments based upon the facts set forth in a hypothetical, case law and general legal principles, which each side would assert for resolution of the issues in their favor. Working through problems will also often disclose gaps in your understanding, of which you were previously unaware. It is worth reemphasizing that the *problem* or *hypothetical* type of legal exam, which includes the Bar, is specifically designed to measure the test-taker's ability to define and discuss issues.

Integrating Syntheses

Step 4 in developing a synthesis is analyzing the inter-relationship of each subchapter, just as you have completed synthesizing and contemplating it, with that which was previously summarized, and then arranging all the data in the appropriate order (i.e. so that each potential issue is considered in a sequential, methodical manner). You must ask yourself not only how the materials of a particular subsection relate to each other, but also, what new aspects of law does the subdivision which has just been completed add to the previously synthesized materials? During the freshman year, this inquiry will usually be answered in one of three ways: *Each subdivision of a casebook (and chapter, too) will represent either (1) an entirely new and distinct cause of action (i.e., theory upon which the defendant can be held liable), (2) another element which must be present (or absent) for a specific cause of action to be successfully maintained, or (3) an exception or defense to a particular cause of action.* Placement of the new data into one of these three categories will determine its position in your evolving synthesis.*

* The answer will be different in some courses. In Civil Procedure, for example, the next subchapter might pertain to another possible defect or omission in pleadings; in Constitutional Law, to another potential basis for upholding or attacking the constitutionality of an enactment.

The second subchapter of the Contracts' casebook is entitled "The Acceptance." It describes various potential problems pertaining to the acceptance of a valid offer. For example, it is often said that the offeree must agree to exactly the terms proposed in the offer, and if these are varied in any respect, the offeree's response is treated as a counter-offer to be accepted or rejected by the party which initially made the offer. However, Section 2-207 of the UCC (under certain circumstances) permits a contract to be formed even though new, additional terms are required by the offeree. Other acceptance problems may arise where (given certain conditions) the offeree neglects to respond to the offer, or where certain actions by the offeree could be construed as acceptance.

The third subchapter describes the problems relating to termination or lapse of an offer. Even though there may have been a valid offer, which is subsequently accepted, an enforceable contract does not exist if some event occurred which caused the offer to become inoperative prior to its acceptance. In such circumstances the acceptance will usually be construed to be a new offer, susceptible to acceptance by the original offeror. Examples of events which cause an offer to terminate are, briefly; rejection (express or implied) by the offeree, the death or dissolution (if a corporation or similar entity) of the offeror, communication of revocation of the offer by the offeror prior to its acceptance, or lapse of a reasonable time (or that period specified for acceptance within the offer).

Once again, the law student must ask himself how does each piece of datum relate to that which preceded it. If a student fails to tie the materials together (i.e., perceive their interrelationship) he will undoubtedly find it very difficult to construct an effective synthesis, and therefore to recall all of the pertinent legal principles during the exam. Thus, a student attempting to correlate the materials contained in the second and third subchapters with those in the first, might reason as follows: A party attempting to escape an undesirable contract would initially contend (whenever possible) that a valid offer had not been made, and even if it had, the offer (for some reason) lapsed or ceased to exist prior to the alleged acceptance, and even if there were a valid offer and it had not terminated, the acceptance was (for some reason) ineffectual; and, finally, even if the formal requisites of an agreement are present, some defense to the enforceability of this particular contract exists. Thus, an abbreviated synthesis of the aforementioned three subchapters of the Contracts' casebook would probably take on the following contours:

The Agreement Process
Was a Valid Offer Communicated to the Offeree?
  (1) Invitation-offer (etc.)
  (2) Definiteness (etc.)
  (3) Writing (etc.)
Did it Terminate Prior to Acceptance?
  (1) Death or dissolution of offeror.
  (2) Rejection by offeree.
  (3) Communication of revocation by offeror to offeree prior to acceptance, unless actual knowledge of revocation by offeree prior to acceptance.
  (4) Lapse of time.
Was There Acceptance?
  (1) Variance of original or additional terms, may be alright under Section 2-207 of UCC.
  (2) Silence (under certain conditions).
  (3) Actions.
Any Exceptions or Defenses to Rule of Enforcing Otherwise Valid Agreement?

(1) Agreement not intended (i.e. joke), and awareness of this fact by other party.

(2) Computation error (where obvious; and no reliance?).

(3) Inability to comprehend legal consequences of actions (i.e., intoxication).

(4) Neither part intended legally binding agreement.

Thus, the second and third subchapters constituted other elements which must be present (or absent) for a contract to be formed. The foregoing demonstration has hopefully permitted the reader to begin to obtain an insight into what is involved in creating a synthesis. You should *not* wait until the last two or three weeks of the semester to commence your syntheses. The process of synthesizing should commence after the initial subchapter is completed and continue throughout the semester. Your syntheses should be rearranged and revised as you comprehend the interrelationship and proper sequence of newly learned principles. The synthesis may even be reduced slightly from time to time as relatively unimportant data is discarded.

Step 5 is to devise and discuss hypotheticals along the lines suggested above each time a synthesis is enlarged.

Another Example of Subchapter Syntheses

Sometimes subchapters will represent an independent cause of action upon which a defendant can be held liable. In the Torts casebook referred to earlier,* there is a chap-

---

* W. Prosser and J. Wade, *Torts, Cases and Materials*, 5th Ed. (Foundation Press, 1971).

ter entitled "Intentional Interference with Person and Property" which contains a subdivision entitled "False Imprisonment." The cases dealing with the latter subject will be reproduced on the following pages. For fun, the reader should derive his own synthesis from the following cases before analyzing the comments which follow.

Torts, Cases and Materials
Chapter 1
Intentional Interference with Person and Property
Section 4. False Imprisonment

BIRD v. *JONES*

Queen's Bench, 1845.
7 A. & E., N.S., 742.

Action for false imprisonment, plaintiff had a verdict, defendant obtained a rule nisi for a new trial.

COLERIDGE, J. This point is, whether certain facts, which may be taken as clear upon the evidence, amount to an imprisonment. These facts, stated shortly, and as I understand them, are in effect as follows:

A part of a public highway was enclosed, and appropriated for spectators of a boat race paying a price for their seats. The plaintiff was desirous of entering this part, and was opposed by the defendant, but after a struggle, during which no momentary detention of his person took place, he succeeded in climbing over the enclosure. Two policemen were then stationed by the defendant to prevent, and they did prevent him from passing onwards in the direction in which he declared his wish to go; but he was allowed to remain unmolested where he was, and was at liberty to go, and was

told that he was so, in the only other direction by which
he could pass. This he refused for some time, and during that time, remained where he had thus placed himself. * * *

But, although thus obstructed, the plaintiff was at
liberty to move his person and go in any other direction, at his free will and pleasure; and no actual force
or restraint on his person was used, unless the obstruction before mentioned amounts to so much.

I lay out of consideration the question of right or
wrong between these parties. The acts will amount to
imprisonment neither more nor less from their being
wrongful or capable of justification. And I am of opinion that there was no imprisonment. To call it so appears to me to confound partial obstruction and disturbance with total obstruction and detention. A
prison may have its boundary large or narrow, visible
or tangible, or, though real, still in the conception
only; it may itself be movable or fixed, but a boundary
it must have; and that boundary the party imprisoned
must be prevented from passing; he must be prevented
from leaving that place, within the ambit of which the
party imprisoning would confine him, except by pris-
on-breach. Some confusion seems to me to arise from
confounding imprisonment of the body with mere loss
of freedom; it is one part of the definition of freedom
to be able to go wheresoever one pleases; but imprisonment is something more than the mere loss of this
power; it includes the notion of restraint within some
limits defined by a will or power exterior to our own.
* * *

On a case of this sort, which, if there be difficulty in
it, is at least purely elementary, it is not easy nor necessary to enlarge; and I am unwilling to put any ex-

treme case hypothetically; but I wish to meet one suggestion, which has been put as avoiding one of the difficulties which cases of this sort might seem to suggest. If it be said that to hold the present case to amount to to an imprisonment would turn every obstruction of the exercise of a right of way into an imprisonment, the answer is, that there must be something like personal menace or force accompanying the act of obstruction, and that, with this, it will amount to imprisonment. I apprehend that is not so. If, in the course of a night, both ends of a street were walled up, and there was no egress from the house but into the street, I should have no difficulty in saying that the inhabitants were thereby imprisoned; but, if only one end were walled up, and an armed force stationed outside to prevent any scaling of the wall or passage that way, I should feel equally clear that there was no imprisonment. If there were, the street would obviously be the prison; and yet, as obviously, none would be confined to it.

[The concurring opinions of WILLIAMS, J., and PATTERSON, J., and the dissenting opinion of DENMAN, C. J., are omitted.]

Rule absolute.

HERRING v. *BOYLE*

Court of Exchequer, 1834.
1 Cr.M. & R. 377.

[Trespass for assault and false imprisonment. Plaintiff, a boy ten years old, had been sent to a school kept by defendant. On December 24 the plaintiff's mother went to the school and asked the defendant to permit the plaintiff to go home with her for a few days. Defendant refused unless the school fees for the quarter ending December 25 were paid. He would not allow the mother to see the boy. On two later occasions the same demand and refusal were repeated. The mother finally sued out a writ of habeas corpus, and obtained the boy's release, seventeen days after her first visit. On these facts the trial court nonsuited the plaintiff. Counsel obtained a rule nisi to set aside the nonsuit, and for a new trial.]

BOLLAND, B. * * * The question is, whether it appears upon the Judge's notes that there was any evidence of a trespass to go to the jury? I am of opinion that there was not, and consequently, that this rule must be discharged. It has been argued on the part of the plaintiff that the misconduct of the defendant amounted to a false imprisonment. I cannot find anything upon the notes of the learned Judge which shews that the plaintiff was at all cognizant of any restraint. There are many cases which shew that it is not necessary, to constitute an imprisonment, that the hand should be laid upon the person; but in no case has any conduct been held to amount to an imprisonment in the absence of the party supposed to be imprisoned. An officer may make an arrest without laying his hand on the party arrested; but in the present case, as far as we know, the boy may have been willing to stay; he does not appear to have been cognizant of any restraint, and there was no evidence of any act whatsoever done by the defendant in his presence. I think that we cannot construe the refusal to the mother in the boy's absence, and without his being cognizant of any restraint, to be an imprisonment of him against his will; and therefore I am of opinion that the rule must be discharged.

Rule discharged.

[The concurring opinions of Alderson, B., and Gurney, B., are omitted.]

STEVENS v. O'NEILL

Supreme Court of New York, Appellate Division, 1900.
51 App.Div. 364, 64 N.Y.S. 663.

VAN BRUNT, P. J. This action was brought to recover damages for an alleged false imprisonment. The answer was, in effect a general denial. The questions raised upon this appeal may be embraced within two classes: First, whether there was evidence enough to justify the jury in finding that there was any false imprisonment; and, second, whether there were any errors committed in the charge of the learned justice who tried the case.

It is claimed upon the part of the appellant that there was no evidence that any restraint was exercised by the defendant or his employees, as against the plaintiff, and that her submission to search was entirely voluntary upon her part. It appears from the evidence of the plaintiff: That she visited the store of the defendant, in the city of New York, on the 15th of December, 1897. That she went to the jewelry counter, and asked the sales girl to show her some watches. The girl showed her some which were very bright in color, and the plaintiff then asked if she had not some more subdued in character, and the girl said, "No." "Then she counted the watches. She said, 'There were so many in the case when I showed them to you. Now,' she says, 'there is one missing.' 'Well,' I said 'probably you have sold the watch'; never thinking she thought I was the thief. Then she sent for the floor walker, and then he sent for the detective, and she said I would have to be searched." The plaintiff repeated the testimony that, when the woman detective came up, she said: "You will have to be searched." That then the detective sent for a man, and they took the plaintiff through the store, between this man and the detective, to the elevator, and went upstairs into a small room, where she was searched. It is claimed upon the part of the appellant that the plaintiff asked to be searched upon the supposition that she was suspected of being the thief, and that she was willing and submitted to search for the purpose of clearing herself from suspicion, and that no restraint whatever was exercised against her by any of the employes of the defendant. It seems to us, when we consider the situation of the plaintiff (that she was in the store of the defendant, surrounded by persons who were employed by the defendant to detect crime, substantially accused of being a thief, and with the statement made to her, "You will have to be searched"), that this was the exercise of such a dominion over her as that the jury might very properly find that restraint was exercised, and that the subsequent proceedings were simply carrying out the threat that they would search her. Under such circumstances the plaintiff certainly was not required to offer physical resistance to this unjustifiable proceeding against her. The jury having resolved this question in her favor, there seems to be no ground whatever for this court to interfere. The authority of the employes of the defendant is established beyond peradventure by the testimony of the defendant himself. These were the agencies employed by him for the protection of his property, and these people, in the proceedings taken by them, were acting clearly within the scope of the authority which had been conferred upon them. * * *

The jury were not bound to find that she went willingly to the room to be searched, simply because she did not actually resist. She was surrounded by superior force, to contend against which was beyond her physical powers, and she had been told what she had to do, and she surrendered unconditionally; and that is all there is as to her submission and willingness to be searched. The jury found such to be the facts, as they probably were. * * *

Judgment and order affirmed.

ASHLAND DRY GOODS CO. v. WAGES

Court of Appeals of Kentucky, 1946.
302 Ky. 577, 195 S.W.2d 312.

DAWSON, JUSTICE. This is an action for false arrest. On the afternoon of April 8, 1944, the appellee, Mrs. Nellie Wages, accompanied by her daughter and two small grandchildren, entered the department store belonging to the appellant, Ashland Dry Goods Company, for the purpose of buying a cap for one of the grandchildren. Mrs. Kemper, a clerk in the store who was known to Mrs. Wages, waited on them and sold Mrs. Wages a cap which, according to Mrs. Wages' testimony, was placed on the baby's head in the presence of Mrs. Kemper. Mrs. Wages removed the cap the child had been wearing, and placed it in her purse. She handed a ten dollar bill to Mrs. Kemper, who went to another part of the store for change. In the meantime, her daughter had taken the other grandchild to the rest room, leaving Mrs. Wages and the baby alone near the counter at which she had made the purchase.

After she received her change Mrs. Wages went to

another part of the store and presumably waited there for her daughter to return. While she was standing there the appellant, Mrs. Mittenthal, manager of the department from which the cap had been purchased, approached Mrs. Wages, and, according to appellee's testimony, said: " 'Lady, give me whatever you put in your purse. Give me your purse so that I can take it out.' I said I didn't take anything and she said: 'Oh, yes, you did, I know better.' I said: 'I did not; I bought a cap and put it on the baby's head and put the old one in my purse.' She said: 'I want your purse so that I can take out whatever you put in it.' By that time my heart was beating so that I couldn't argue with her. Question: What did she do? Answer: She argued with me and said: 'You cannot leave the store, that is orders.' And I started walking off and she followed me and I said I didn't take anything and she reached over and jerked my purse and took it over to the end of the counter and this girl that reported me was standing there and she unzipped the purse and she took the cap out and laid it down. She didn't give it to anybody. She went on through my purse and I had the little girl sitting there on the counter. I was ready to go down but I knew if I did she would put something in there and say I took it." Mrs. Mittenthal took the old cap from the purse and placed it in a bag and returned it to the appellee.

It appears from the evidence that one of the clerks in the store (not Mrs. Kemper) saw Mrs. Wages place the old cap in her purse and informed still another clerk of what she had seen and asked her advice as to what to do. She was advised to report the incident to Mrs. Mittenthal, which she did, and this resulted in the

investigation and the incident which is the basis for
this action.   *   *   *

[A verdict for plaintiff in the first trial was set aside
because it made no separation as to compensatory and
punitive damages. On the second trial the jury returned
a verdict for plaintiff for $100 compensatory and $700
punitive damages. Defendant appeals, assigning various errors, including the denial of its motion for a directed verdict.]

It is vigorously argued that the acts of Mrs. Mittenthal do not constitute a false arrest or an unlawful detention of the appellee. In determining this question we
must accept the appellee's version of the affair. It is
contended that the transactions as recited by the appellee do not amount to false imprisonment, the theory
being that appellee was in no way restrained and was
at liberty to go her way. We are unable to agree with
this contention since, although appellee probably was
at liberty to leave the store at any time, and there is
no evidence that she was forcibly restrained from doing
so, the result of her departure would have been an
automatic parting with her purse. It is natural to assume that the appellee, knowing her innocence, was
most reluctant to leave the store without her purse
and its contents. We are of the opinion that the reten-
tion of the purse and the statement by Mrs. Mittenthal
that the appellee could not leave the store until the
package was wrapped constituted an unlawful detention without her consent and against her will, and that
the court properly submitted this question to the jury.
*   *   *

[The judgment for $100 compensatory damages was
affirmed, but as to the $700 punitive damages, it was
reversed, on the ground that there was no evidence

that the defendant's employee was acting maliciously, or with any evil motive.]

MARTIN v. HOUCK

Supreme Court of North Carolina, 1906.
141 N.C. 317, 54 S.E. 291.

The action was brought to recover damages for an unlawful arrest and false imprisonment. The defendant, Calvin Houck, was a policeman of Granite Falls, when he was informed that the plaintiff had stolen a pair of shoes from a store while it was on fire. He and his codefendants, J. O. Deal and George Lefevers, who acted as deputies, went to the plaintiff's house, which was two miles from the town, in the night and after the plaintiff and his wife had retired, and arrested him, after searching the house at plaintiff's request, as the state's evidence tended to show. The plaintiff's wife was compelled to dress in the presence of these strangers. The plaintiff, when accused of stealing the shoes, denied his guilt, but voluntarily agreed to go with the defendants to town and answer the charge. The defendants then told him that he need not go that night if he would come to town the next morning, which he promised to do. He went to Granite Falls the next morning, but no warrant was ever issued, and no accusation made against him for stealing the shoes.

[No formal charge had been made against plaintiff, and the defendants had no warrant. The officer was acting outside of the town of Granite Falls, and had no authority to arrest the plaintiff. The trial court refused defendants' request for an instruction which would in effect direct a verdict in their favor, and left to the jury the question whether plaintiff was in fact arrested. The jury found that defendants had unlawfully arrested plaintiff, and returned a verdict in his favor for $200, upon which judgment was entered. Defendants appeal.]

WALKER, J. * * * There was abundant evidence to show that the plaintiff had been unduly restrained of his liberty by Houck, and the other defendants who were present and participated. In ordinary practice, words are sufficient to constitute an imprisonment, if they impose a restraint upon the person, and the party is accordingly restrained; for he is not obliged to incur the risk of personal violence and insult by resisting until actual violence be used. This principle is reasonable in itself, and is fully sustained by the authorities. Nor does it seem that there should be any very formal declaration of arrest. If the officer goes for the purpose of executing his warrant, and has the party in his presence and power, if the party so understands it, and in consequence thereof submits, and the officer, in the execution of the warrant, takes the party before a magistrate, or receives money or property in discharge of his person, it is in law an arrest, although he did not touch any part of the body. It is not necessary to constitute false imprisonment that the person restrained of his liberty should be touched or actually arrested. If he is ordered to do or not to do the thing, to move or not to move against his own free will, if it is not left to his option to go or stay where he pleases, and force is offered, or there is reasonable ground to apprehend that coercive measures will be used if he does not yield, the offense is complete upon his submission. A false imprisonment may be committed by words alone, or by acts alone, or by both, and by merely operating on the will of the individual, or by personal violence, or by both. It is not necessary that the individual be confined within a prison or within walls, or that he be assaulted. It may be committed by threats. [Citation omitted.] The evidence shows that the defendant Houck said to the plaintiff: "Consider yourself under arrest. You must go back to Granite Falls with us." Plaintiff asked for his warrant, when Houck replied: "That is all right about the warrant. You must go to Granite Falls with us." Plaintiff then said: "I will go with you." There was still other evidence showing that he submitted to the control they attempted to exercise over his person and that he was made to act contrary to his own will. It is clear, we think, that there was no error in the charge with respect to the question whether or not there was an arrest. * * * We can find no error in the rulings and charge of the court.

No error.

WHITTAKER v. SANDFORD

Supreme Judicial Court of Maine, 1912.
110 Me. 77, 85 A. 399.

[Plaintiff was a member of a religious sect, of which defendant was the leader. The sect had a colony at Jaffa, in Syria, which plaintiff had joined. Plaintiff decided to abandon the movement and to return to America. Defendant asked her to come back to America on his yacht rather than by steamer; and when plaintiff suggested that she might not be let off of the yacht until she was "won to the movement again," defendant assured her repeatedly that under no circumstances would she be detained on board. Plaintiff accepted the assurance and sailed for America on the yacht. On arrival in port defendant refused to furnish her with a boat so that she could leave the yacht. She remained on board for nearly a month, and finally obtained her release by a writ of habeas corpus. She brought an action for false imprisonment. The jury returned a verdict in her favor for $1100. Defendant excepted to the court's instructions, and appeals from an order denying his motion for a new trial.]

SAVAGE, J.   *   *   *   The court instructed the jury that the plaintiff to recover must show that the restraint was physical, and not merely a moral influence; that it must have been actual physical restraint, in the sense that one intentionally locked into a room would be physically restrained but not necessarily involving physical force upon the person; that it was not necessary that the defendant, or any person by his direction, should lay his hand upon the plaintiff; that if the plaintiff was restrained so that she could not leave the yacht Kingdom by the intentional refusal to furnish transportation as agreed, she not having it in her power to escape otherwise, it would be a physical restraint and unlawful imprisonment. We think the instructions were apt and sufficient. If one should, without right, turn the key in a door, and thereby prevent a person in the room from leaving, it would be the simplest form of unlawful imprisonment. The restraint is physical. The four walls and the locked door are physical impediments to escape. Now is it different when one who is in control of a vessel at anchor, within practical rowing distance from the shore, who has agreed that a guest on board shall be free to leave, there being no means to leave except by rowboats, wrongfully refuses the guest the use of a boat? The boat is the key. By refusing the boat he turns the key. The guest is as effectually locked up as if there were walls along the sides of the vessel. The restraint is physical. The impassable sea is the physical barrier.

A careful study of the evidence leads us to conclude that the jury were warranted in finding that the defendant was guilty of unlawful imprisonment. This, to be sure, is not an action based upon the defendant's failure to keep his agreement to permit the plaintiff to leave the yacht as soon as it should reach shore. But his duty under the circumstances is an important consideration. It cannot be believed that either party to the agreement understood that it was his duty merely to bring her to an American harbor. The agreement implied that she was to go ashore. There was no practical way for her to go ashore except in the yacht's boats. The agreement must be understood to mean that he would bring her to land, or to allow her to get to land, by the only available means. The evidence is that he refused her a boat. His refusal was wrongful. The case leaves not the slightest doubt that he had the power to control the boats, if he chose to exercise it. It was not enough for him to leave it to the husband to say whether she might go ashore or not. She had a personal right to go on shore. If the defendant personally denied her the privilege, as the jury might find he did, it was a wrongful denial.

The holdings of the foregoing cases (including a few additional notes pertaining to *escape*) would yield statements such as the following:

A false imprisonment results when one is intentionally confined to a definable area against his will.

Plaintiff is not obliged to attempt an escape where there

is a reasonable possibility of injury to his person or property.

A means of escape which is not reasonably apparent is no escape at all.

The plaintiff must be aware of his imprisonment to assert a cause of action (unless injured during his confinement; Restatement of Torts, 42).

Where plaintiff (a woman) is surrounded by defendant's employees and told "you will have to be searched," plaintiff's compliance was against her will.

Where plaintiff was ordered not to leave the premises and defendant refused to return plaintiff's property (her purse), plaintiff was restrained against her will.

Where plaintiff was threatened with bodily injury by law officers unless he complied with their orders, he was restrained against his will. Rationale—One need not suffer physical injury to prove the restraint was against his will.

A threat of future action (i.e., "If you don't remain here, I'll call police") is not a sufficient restraint.

A plaintiff must be physically (as opposed to psychologically or mentally) confined to have a cause of action (but this was dictum—plaintiff was, in fact, physically restrained).

A synthesis of the opinions reproduced above could be the following:

A false imprisonment occurs where

(1) The defendant *intentionally*, and

(2) *against plaintiff's will* (implicit in his issue is the question of whether the plaintiff was reasonable in feeling constrained under the circumstances)—*Yes*, where (i) plaintiff, a woman, is surrounded and told she would have to be searched, (ii) plaintiff, a woman, ordered not to leave, purse withheld, and (iii) plaintiff threatened with bodily

harm by law officers if didn't obey. (R—one need not actually incur physical violence to prove restraint was involuntary). . . . No, where (i) threat of future action, (ii) restraint must be physical (as opposed to psychological or mental)—but this was dictum,

(3) restricts plaintiff's movements to a *definable* area,

(4) from which there was no reasonable or apparent *escape*, and

(5) plaintiff is *aware* of his situation (unless injured).

The characteristics of an effective synthesis are present once again. The Torts cause of action called *false imprisonment* has been synthesized and dissected into its basic components. Approximately 11 pages of text have been reduced into 5 distinguishable elements (and 15 lines), thereby enhancing the likelihood that the potential issues inherent in a false imprisonment question will be remembered during the final exam. The significant facts and dictum are contained immediately after the proposition of law to which they pertain. Finally, case names have been omitted from this summary because memorization of them is not ordinarily expected by the grader.

Analyzing the synthesis of false imprisonment for the purpose of flagging the words or phrases which would be likely sources of issues on an exam, you would probably reason as follows: Whether the confinement was intentional should be fairly obvious;* whether plaintiff's freedom of movement was restricted to a definable area would also seem to be fairly easy to determine; however, the question of whether plaintiff's will had been overcome by defend-

---

* Of course, someone could accidentally restrain another (i.e., locking a department store with an unnoticed customer inside), but such a situation would present a negligence rather than false imprisonment problem.

ant's words and/or actions has been a recurring issue, and
therefore will probably appear in a hypothetical involving
false imprisonment; whether a "reasonable" or "apparent"
escape was available to plaintiff is also a likely source of
controversy since terms such as these lend themselves to
the argumentative process; finally, whether plaintiff is
cognizant of his confinement should be obvious.

Again, the next step is to imagine *several* situations
which explore the parameters of the formulation. For example, what if plaintiff, while waiting for a bus was accosted by defendant (an ominous looking fellow who had
both his hands in his jacket pockets) and told that he would
be stabbed if he boarded the bus which was about to arrive? Plaintiff remains still, and after the bus leaves defendant simply walks away. Would defendant's actions constitute false imprisonment?

There is no doubt that the defendant intended to restrict
plaintiff's movement, and was successful. The first real
issue would be whether the plaintiff justifiably felt constrained to remain at the bus stop (i.e., was plaintiff's will
overcome?). Plaintiff could contend that under the circumstances he was entitled to believe the defendant would carry
out his threat and could cite decisions stating that one need
not actually incur bodily harm to prove that he had not
acted voluntarily. In rebuttal defendant would argue that
since a knife had never been manifested, and he had threatened only future action, plaintiff's inaction was not coerced;
and that a restraint must be physical, as opposed to mental, in nature. Also, defendant would contend that plaintiff was not limited to a definable area (since he could advance in any direction except toward the bus) and could
have escaped by simply running down the street. Plaintiff's
response would be that the spirit of defendant's remarks
and the context in which they were made would lead a

reasonable person to believe he would be attacked if he did anything but remain absolutely still; nor did plaintiff have an apparent escape, because defendant might have chased and overtaken him if he had attempted to flee from the area.

The next step would once again be analyzing the inter-relationship of the course materials. The subchapters preceding and following "False Imprisonment" are entitled "Assault" and "Infliction of Emotional Distress," respectively. The reader would find that these subdivisions represent *independent* grounds upon which a defendant could be held liable for his conduct. Thus, a synthesis of this area of Torts law ("Intentional Interference With Person and Property") should clearly indicate that assault, false imprisonment, and infliction of emotional distress are independent, distinct causes of action (as opposed to elements or components of a single cause of action). As mentioned earlier, new materials sometimes represent exceptions or defenses to specific causes of action. Even if all of the elements of a false imprisonment could be proved, subsequent opinions in the casebook would indicate that no recovery could be obtained if, for example, the defendant reasonably believed the restraint was necessary to prevent plaintiff from attempting to murder him. Thus, a subsection (6) entitled "Defenses" could be added at the conclusion of a synthesis on intentional torts, under which the words *Self-Defense* would be inserted. The next task, of course, would be to devise hypotheticals containing as many of the issues inherent in the synthesized materials as possible.

The Evolving Synthesis

Understanding the interrelationship of briefed materials

and perceiving the manner in which the potential issues contained in such information could arise on an exam hypothetical are essential ingredients to creating effective syntheses. To reiterate, an *effective synthesis is one in which the various principles and doctrines of a course are arranged in the order in which the potential issues they represent would arise in a factual situation which contained all of such issues.* It should be emphasized that the term *order* is not intended to imply that each issue would have a unique place upon a time line. Where several doctrines or causes of action are supported by a single set of facts (which is often the case), each of the doctrines or actions and the issues inherent therein would be applicable concurrently. However, the potential issues inherent in each doctrine and cause of action can be arranged to facilitate consideration of them in a relatively logical, systematic manner. Thus, for each cause of action your synthesis would clearly indicate (i) the necessary elements, (ii) each possible defense to it, (iii) each possible exception to such defenses, and (iv) from whom and for what injuries could a successful plaintiff recover.

The conventional freshman synthesis usually follows the casebook's table of contents. This is unfortunate because the elements of, defenses and exceptions to a particular doctrine or cause of action often appear under separate chapter or subchapter headings. For example, *causation in fact* and *proximate cause* are essential elements to the maintenance of a single cause of action—*negligence*; yet "Negligence," "Causation in Fact" and "Proximate Cause" are each treated under *independent* chapters in the Torts' casebook mentioned earlier. Likewise, although an enforceable contract does not arise unless legally adequate *consideration* is present, this topic is *not* included in the chapter entitled "The Agreement Process." Similarly, the previous discussion pertaining to the materials found in the Contracts' casebook chapter called "The Agreement Process" revealed that some of those cases were concerned with defenses to the enforcement of a valid contract. *Thus, a casebook's table of contents is often inconsistent with understanding the interrelationship of the course materials and consideration of the principles inherent in a specific doctrine or cause of action in a logical, sequential order.*

Instead of one lengthy synthesis which has been drafted to correspond to the table of contents found in the casebook, it is usually more practical to break the course down into several major areas, for each of which there will be a separate synthesis. (There are usually no more than seven to eight.) The determination of major areas should be made along functional lines (i.e., which causes of action or doctrines are likely to be found in a single set of facts). Again, illustrations are warranted. One of the hypotheticals on a typical law school Torts exam may (and often does) contain issues involving the independent intentional torts of assault, battery, false imprisonment and conversion. The reason this occurs is because the material facts which give rise to these causes of action overlap to a great extent. On the other hand, it would be unlikely for the same hypothetical which contained the foregoing intentional torts to also include a cause of action against the defendant for defamation, since *numerous* additional facts would have to be present. Thus, "Intentional Torts to Persons and/or Property" might be one major area and "Defamation" another. Similarly, in Contracts, the facts which ordinarily give rise to an agreement process hypothetical may be quite different from those involved in a parol evidence problem, and therefore each topic would be a distinct major area.

The foregoing should not be taken to suggest that two or more major areas are never found in the same hypothetical. The opposite is true. In a Torts' exam, for example, privacy and defamation questions are frequently contained within the same hypothetical. However, because the factual elements of each of these independent causes of action are relatively distinct, it would be unwieldy to consider them both under a single major area heading. Similarly, while the given facts in a Contracts' hypothetical may contain agreement process and quasi-contract problems, it would be impractical to include these subjects within the same major area.

As you comprehend the interrelationship of newly learned principles to preceding materials, you will probably be obliged to reorganize your syntheses several times throughout the semester. After each chapter and subdivision is briefed and synthesized, you should ask— how does the doctrine or subject just learned pertain to the principles already assimilated? The answer to this question will determine the appropriate place to insert the new data into the synthesis. As noted above, the materials pertaining to a particular subject may be scattered throughout the casebook under different chapter and subdivision headings. The inconvenience and time devoted to modifying your syntheses as the interrelationship of topics and principles is perceived is well spent since the checklists described on the following pages are merely outlines lifted from the syntheses.

Summary

The importance of *understanding* the interrelationship of the course materials cannot be overemphasized. It is only *after* this is accomplished that you will be able to anticipate the context in which the issues inherent in all of the topics could arise on a law school exam. An effective synthesis is one that is organized so that the issues inherent in the elements and doctrines of which each major area is composed will be considered in a methodical, systematic manner. To achieve this end you must continually revise your syntheses so that each piece of information is inserted into the appropriate niche.

The Checklist

Definition and Illustration of the Checklist

The procedure which facilitates the spotting of issues in hypothetical problems has been referred to earlier as the *checklist method*. Actually, there will be several checklists for each course, one for each of the major areas. *The great thing about checklists, which are simply outlines lifted from the synthesis of a particular course, is that so long as you recognize the applicability of a major area to the hypothetical problem you will systematically consider each potential issue within such area.* Spotting and defining the issues is the most important aspect of any hypothetical type of legal exam. As one of my professors once told me: "If an attorney sees the issues, he can always look up the law; if he doesn't, valuable rights may be lost forever." It is only *after* the issues are defined that all of the pro and con arguments for their resolution can be made.

The best way to explain a *checklist* is by means of an illustration. One of the major topics in Torts law is negligence. A checklist which I devised for this subject when studying for the California Bar is set forth below. It is somewhat abbreviated in that every possible sub-issue under each of the major elements has not been included. Nevertheless, the checklist still represents a legitimate one-page condensation of the major points contained in the 240 pages of the Torts casebook referred to earlier.*

* W. Prosser and J. Wade, *Torts, Cases and Materials*, 5th Ed. (Foundation Press, 1971).

Negligence Checklist

Standard—r. person (custom, kn, emerg'y)
(children, professionals, mental)

Proof
- (1) R.I.L. (res ipsa loquitur)
  - (a) Unlikely) presumption
  - (b) no c.n.) or
  - (c) exclusive control) inference
- (2) Statutes
  - (a) define standard of conduct) presumption,
  - (b) intended to prevent that) inference,
    type of injury) per se
  - (c) class protected)

Actual Causation (causation in fact)

Duty

Unforeseeable Consequences (proximate cause)

Defenses
- (1) C.N. (Contributory Neg.)
- (2) AOR (Assumption of Risk) − kn + vol'y
  But defenses may be nullified if
  - (a) L.C.C. ("Last Clear Chance") Kn./ability, or
  - (b) Wantonness

Damages
- (1) hit
- (2) avoidable consequences
- (3) past–future (medi, wages, mental suffering)

    (4) exemplary/recklessness
    (5) companionship

Who is liable, for what
    (1) vicarious liability (er-ee; jt enterprises, etc.)
    (2) contribution rights

The checklist indicates that there are five basic elements to a negligence action: The defendant must have acted negligently; the defendant's actions must have been both the actual cause (causation in fact) and proximate cause (unforeseeable consequences) of plaintiff's injury; the defendant must have been under a legal duty not to expose plaintiff to risk of physical injury; and the plaintiff must have been damaged (either personally or to his property) as a result of defendant's actions. The checklist also indicates that two possible means of proving that the defendant acted negligently, depending on the circumstances, are showing that (i) the doctrine of res ipsa loquitur is applicable, or (ii) the defendant's conduct violated a penal or civil statute. The checklist also discloses that there are two main defenses to a negligence action—contributory negligence and assumption of risk; unless a doctrine which nullifies the defense is also present (such as last clear chance or recklessness). Finally, assuming that plaintiff prevailed on the foregoing points, you would next consider from whom and in what amounts recovery could be made, and any rights of the tortfeasors against each other.

Turning to a more extended discussion of the principles mentioned above, an initial question in the determination of whether or not one has acted in a negligent manner is whether that party's conduct has fallen below the *standard* by which he (or it) is to be judged. The test for an ordinary person is usually phrased something like, "Did the defendant act like a reasonable person under the circumstances?" To give an extreme example, if while running to catch a train a man inadvertently charges into an elderly woman, knocking her down and causing her serious injury, a jury could certainly find that he had not acted reasonably under the circumstances (i.e. the importance of catching a train does not justify undertaking the risk of causing physical injury to another). But, if the same accident had occurred while the defendant was pursuing someone whom he had just seen commit a multiple homicide, then there would be an excellent possibility that the jury would not consider the defendant to have acted unreasonably under the circumstances (i.e., the importance of apprehending a murderer does justify the accidental harm caused to a bystander).

To the immediate right of "Standard" are the terms *custom, kn.,* and *emerg'y.* The word *custom* is a shorthand way of referring to the legal principle that a particular act or omission may be deemed negligent even though it is commonly committed or omitted by an entire industry or profession (i.e., failure of the tire manufacturers to test their products prior to sale). *Kn.* (knowledge) stands for the proposition that all persons are considered to have certain basic general knowledge (i.e., that ice is slippery). The word *emerg'y* (emergency) is a reference to the proposition that conduct otherwise unreasonable might be considered "reasonable under the circumstances" when the alleged tortfeasor has been placed under great stress (i.e., a driver leaping from his moving taxicab when a firearm is suddenly pointed at him by one of his passengers).

Immediately below the foregoing terms are the words, *children, professionals,* and *mental. Children* who commit allegedly tortious acts are usually judged by the criterion of what would be reasonable for a child of like age, intelligence and experience. *Professionals* (i.e., doctors and attorneys) are ordinarily held to the level of competence usually exercised by members of that profession in the same or similar locations. Individuals with a *mental* disability are usually held to the "reasonable person" test, despite their deficiency.

All of the aforementioned terms could have been extracted from opinions in the subsection entitled "Standard of Care" of the Torts casebook mentioned earlier.* Each of these standards would have been set out completely on the synthesis, but as they were understood and memorized a mere word or two sufficed to facilitate their recollection on the checklist. Abbreviations are utilized because a student who is not permitted to take notes into the exam will want to re-create the checklist as rapidly as possible. Case names have been omitted since most professors do not expect students to cite specific opinions on the exam.

The topics dealing with *Proof* of negligence are divided into two sections: *R.I.L.* (res ipsa loquitur) and *Statutes.* Res ipsa loquitur ("the event speaks for itself") represents a means of establishing negligence when it is impossible or very difficult for a plaintiff to obtain direct evidence of the incident which resulted in injury (i.e., a plane crashing and disintegrating while attempting a landing on a clear day). Ordinarily three factors must be present for this doctrine to be applied; the accident must be a type which is *unlikely* to occur unless there has been negligence, there must have been *no contributory negligence* on the part of the plaintiff, and the instrumentality which caused the injury must have been under the defendant's *exclusive control.* While most courts treat res ipsa loquitur as creating only

---

* W. Prosser and J. Wade, *Torts, Cases and Materials*, 5th Ed. (Foundation Press, 1971).

an *inference* of negligence, a few have stated that it constitutes a *rebuttable presumption.**

The term *Statutes* suggests the general rule that where a defendant, as a result of some violation of a penal statute, injures plaintiff, the plaintiff may assert defendant's failure to conform to such statute as proof of negligence. However, before the statute can be deemed applicable, the plaintiff must usually show that it (1) clearly defined a standard of conduct which the defendant did not meet, (2) was intended to prevent the type of injury that occurred, and (3) plaintiff was within the class which the statute attempted to protect. The effect which an applicable statute will be given varies from state to state. Usually it creates a presumption or inference of negligence, however, a few jurisdictions observe a *per se* rule.

Actual causation is an allusion to the principle that the negligence must have been the *but for* cause of the injury. For example, if the defendant (the builder of a dam which broke due to overfilling because of a torrential downpour) can show that, although the dam was negligently constructed, even a properly built dam would have given way due to the increased pressure resulting from the storm, defendant's negligence would *not* have been the actual cause of the injuries which followed after the dam burst (i.e., the plaintiff's negligence was not the *but for* cause of the injuries and damage which followed since they would have occurred anyway).

A grossly over-simplified description of *duty* refers to the concept that the parties must have stood in such a relationship to each other so that the plaintiff was under a legal obligation to not expose the defendant to risk of injury. Once again on a superficial plane, *unforeseeable conse-*

---

* An explanation of these terms will be left to the reader's formal legal education.

quences stands for the proposition that where the extent of the injury and the manner in which it came about were (in hindsight) unforeseeable in the ordinary course of events, the defendant will not be held to have been negligent. An example illustrating both of these doctrines could be the following: Mr. A, who had just purchased forty sticks of dynamite, tripped over a hose which the defendant had negligently left on the public walkway outside his residential home, with the result that a tremendous explosion occurred, which in turn caused the priceless antique being exhibited for one day in another home two blocks away to topple and shatter; and the ex-owner of the valuable item sues the defendant. The damage to plaintiff's antique, it could be argued, was not within the physical proximity of the likely type of risk the hose presented (i.e., someone slipping and breaking a leg), so plaintiff had no *duty* to the defendant. The foregoing also illustrates *unforeseeable consequences* since the manner in which the damage occurred, and the extent of the loss, were both extraordinary.

Under the word *defenses* is the term *Contributory Negligence* (CN). This refers to the proposition of law that one party cannot recover from another where the former's negligence was also partially responsible for the incident which resulted in injury. The letters *AOR* stand for the doctrine called *Assumption of Risk*. For a defendant to successfully maintain this defense, it must be shown not only that plaintiff was actually (or should have been) aware of the risk of harm, but also that he voluntarily chose to undertake that risk. For example, if the plaintiff chooses to walk up several flights of stairs to his apartment, even though he is aware that some of the steps are weak, and there is an elevator in working order which can take him to his destination, and he is subsequently injured when one of the steps collapses, the defendant would certainly assert *AOR* as a defense.

Immediately below the above-mentioned defenses, are the terms *last clear chance* (*LCC*) and *recklessness*. A description of the *last clear chance* doctrine would be the following: Mr. A, driving a car, sees Mr. B crossing in the middle of the street in front of him, but does not slow down because A calculates that if each maintains their present speed, no contact will result; unfortunately, B suddenly stumbled and is struck by A's vehicle; while B was contributorily negligent in crossing in the middle of the street, A was aware of B's situation and had the ability to avoid the accident, but did not; therefore, *LCC* is applicable and B's contributory negligence will not prevent a recovery from A. The terms *Kn./ability* to the right of *LCC* indicate that plaintiff must show that the defendant had actual knowledge of plaintiff's predicament (although some jurisdictions require only that the defendant should have been aware of it), and that the defendant had the ability to avoid mishap (although some courts have held that where the defendant's antecedent negligence has deprived him of this ability the defendant will be deemed to have had such ability). The reason *LCC* was placed immediately after *CN* is because if the latter doctrine is applicable, the next question which would have to be examined is the possible applicability of the former (since *LCC*, in effect, negates *CN*).

Finally, *wantonness* stands for the principle that where the defendant exhibited a reckless disregard for the safety of others, the plaintiff's contributory negligence may also be nullified. Thus, where the defendant, while speeding down a city street and talking to his passenger, hits the plaintiff (who was crossing against a red light), plaintiff might still be able to successfully maintain a negligence action against the defendant as a result of the latter's disregard of the risk of serious injury to others despite his own negligence. *LCC* probably would not be applicable since the defendant may have never seen the plaintiff, or would not have had the ability to stop in time if he had.

Under the heading of *damages*, the term *hit* refers to the general rule that the defendant's negligent conduct must have resulted in some type (regardless of how slight) of physical impact upon the plaintiff. *Avoidable consequences* is a shorthand way of stating the principle that the plaintiff cannot recover for damages which could have been avoided (i.e., refusing medical attention and thereby aggravating his injuries). The words *past/future, med., wages, mental suffering* stand for the proposition that a successful plaintiff is entitled to recover not only for lost wages, medical expenses and mental anguish incurred through the trial, but also for similar damages which will probably be suffered in the future. A plaintiff is usually not permitted to recover *exemplary* (or punitive) damages in a negligent suit, but exceptions have been made where the defendant exhibited a *reckless* disregard for the safety of others. *Companionship* refers to the minority view which allows recovery for the emotional loss which occurs when a member of one's immediate family is seriously injured or killed.

The last major topic, *Who Is Liable, For What*, pertains to the cluster of problems which become relevant after negligence has been established. *Vicarious liability* suggests the doctrine whereby a party (or entity) can be held liable for the negligence of another. For example, a corporate employer is usually liable for injuries inflicted through the negligence of its employees in the conduct of its business. Similarly, all the participants of *joint venture* may be liable for the negligent acts or omissions of any one of them in furtherance of the common undertaking. Finally, where joint and severally liable defendants have *contribution rights* among themselves, each can sue the others for the latter's proportionate share of the judgment.

While the brief, highly over-simplified description of the doctrines and principles pertaining to negligence mentioned above leaves much to be desired, a better understanding of the checklist concept should have been gleaned from the foregoing discussion. *By organizing a course into a relatively few major areas, and distilling these down to an outline which contains the important topics within each of such areas, you will find that your analysis of a hypothetical which contains said area will proceed in a methodical, systematic manner.* Provided you recognize the applicability of a major area to a particular hypothetical, the checklists should greatly minimize the possibility that you may overlook non-conspicuous issues. Checklists, like syntheses, should be subjected to continuous modification. If you are confident that you can recall the subprinciples of a particular element, or that some principles are relatively unimportant, these can be omitted from the checklists you ultimately use.

An Example Demonstrating the Use of a Checklist on an Examination

Although it would be miraculous if the reader were able to acquire an understanding of negligence on the basis of the brief remarks above, an understanding of the checklist method would probably be enhanced by an illustration of the interaction between a checklist and an actual question.

The following instructions and hypothetical problem pertaining to negligence appeared on the 1972 California Bar Examination (summer session):

Instructions

"An answer should demonstrate your ability to analyze the facts presented by the question, to select the material from the immaterial facts, and discern the points upon which the case turns. It should show your knowledge and understanding of the pertinent principles and theories of law, their relationship to each other, and their qualifications and limitations. It should evidence your ability to apply the law to the facts given, and to reason logically in a lawyer-like manner to a sound conclusion from the premises adopted. Try to demonstrate your proficiency in using and applying legal principles rather than a mere memory of them.

"An answer containing only a statement of your conclusions will receive little credit. State fully the reasons that support them. All points should be thoroughly discussed. Although your answer should be complete, you should not volunteer information or discuss legal doctrines that are not necessary or pertinent to the solution of the problem.

QUESTION NO. 2

"An unprecedented storm in the city of X caused the flooding of the city's conduits under a public street. This caused the electrical wiring that controlled a traffic signal at a nearby intersection to become short circuited. As a result, a green "go" light was continuously displayed both to north-south and east-west traffic. When this confusing situation first occurred, a city policeman observed it but did nothing to extinguish the green light or to provide any warning at the intersection.

"Two hours later the lights were still green for all

traffic. Peter, driving his car north bound, observed the green light and proceeded directly toward the intersection. At the same time, Saul, who was operating his car in violation of a criminal statute prohibiting driving while being intoxicated, approached the intersection heading west. Saul saw the "go" signal facing him and proceeded to cross. He assumed that Peter's car, which he saw approaching from the south, would be brought to a halt as it approached what Saul presumed must be a "red" signal. Peter, in turn, saw Saul as the latter proceeded into the intersection. Peter made an effort to stop and could have done so if the brake fluid in his car's master cylinder had not been too low. A reasonable inspection would have disclosed that his brakes were defective for this reason. In the collision that followed, Saul's car was struck broadside and injuries were sustained by both Peter and Saul.

A state statute subjects a municipality to liability for negligence to the same extent that a private corporation for profit would be liable under the same circumstances."

"Discuss possible liabilities of the city and of each driver."

Since the bottom line of the question requests the test-taker to discuss the possible liabilities of all of the parties, there could be four lawsuits: Peter (P) v. City of X (X), P v. Saul (S), S v. X, and S v. P. Recognizing that the hypothetical involves negligence issues, the student would work his way down the checklist in the following manner.

In P's suit against X, a threshold issue would be, "Did X (through its representative, the policeman) act reasonably under the circumstances?" Since the electrical short-circuit was caused by an "unprecedented" storm, it would be difficult to successfully argue that X was negligent by failing to maintain traffic signals which subsequently did not operate properly. However, the policeman probably did not act reasonably, in view of the obvious danger of a car collision and the loss of life which could follow, when he did not remain at the intersection to direct traffic, or at least attempt to correct the situation by calling another officer immediately. The fact that such an exceedingly hazardous condition was allowed to exist for two hours indicates that X had fallen below the standard required of it under the circumstances.

The next prospective issue would be a contention by X that the malfunctioning traffic light was not the actual cause of the accident, but rather S's operation of an automobile while intoxicated. P's response to this would be that (1) the accident would not have occurred *but for* X's negligence with regard to the traffic light, and (2) even if S were negligent also, X and S would simply be joint tortfeasors, each being fully liable for the full damages (although P could only obtain one recovery).

X could next argue that since the injuries occurred as the result of a chain of *unforeseeable consequences* (each driver noticing the other, but one being drunk and the other unable to stop his vehicle), all of the necessary elements of negligence are not present. At this point, the test-taker should probably make an explicit assumption that, "Although S was intoxicated, the hypothetical discloses nothing that would indicate that S's inebriated condition affected his driving (that S was speeding, or that his thought processes or reflexes were impaired). It will thus be assumed that S's drunkenness is irrelevant." Also, it was not so *unforeseeable* that a motorist would be unable to avoid a collision as a result of his inability to stop his car; brakes fail for a variety of reason (be it the result of wet streets or defective parts). Finally, P would contend that the way in which the accident occurred (both parties being aware of the other) was not so extraordinary as to make the *unforeseeable consequences* doctrine applicable, and therefore preclude P's negligence action.

X would next contend that P was contributorily negligent in not having made a reasonable inspection of the brake fluid in his car. P's response would be that the typical reasonably prudent person does not open up his car's master cylinder to check the brake fluid each time he decides to drive somewhere. The mere fact that a "reasonable inspection" would have disclosed this situation, is not conclusive that it was unreasonable for P to not have dismantled part of his car's engine before starting out.

Assuming P prevailed on all of the foregoing points, the question of the extent of damages he would be capable of recovering would be the next consideration. However, this topic will be discussed after the possible liability of each defendant is examined.

P would probably also bring a negligence action against S. Again, a threshold issue would be, "Did S act like a reasonable person under the circumstances?" Based upon the assumption made above (i.e. that S's violation of the criminal statute prohibited driving while intoxicated was not connected with the injury, and therefore is not applicable), P would have a difficult time proving that S had not acted reasonably. It is quite natural for a driver to presume if he has a "go" signal, a driver coming from a perpendicular angle would have a "red" signal. However, P would contend that whereas S's presumption might be reasonable under ordinary circumstances, an ordinarily prudent person would realize that a torrential rainstorm might affect traffic lights, and therefore would not make the ordinary assumption that the signal facing an intersecting driver is functioning.

S might raise *actual causation, unforeseeable consequences* and *contributory negligence*. However, since these problems were discussed in the context of P's suit against X, it need not be reiterated.

In S's lawsuit against X, the same issues would arise which occurred in P's suit against X. Of course, however, the *contributory negligence* issue would take on a different aspect. X would contend that S's violation of the criminal statute prohibited driving while intoxicated constituted contributory negligence on P's part, and therefore his recovery is barred. Based upon the facts presumed above, however, X would probably have a difficult time in sustaining this issue.

In S's lawsuit against P, most of the same issues which were present in P's lawsuit against S would recur. However, S would probably contend that even if there had been contributory negligence on his part, such negligence would be nullified since P had the *last clear chance*. S's argument would be that because P was aware of S's negligence (i.e., proceeding through what was apparently a red light), and would have had the ability to stop and thereby avoid the accident were it not for P's antecedent negligence, any contributory negligence of S is negated. In rebuttal, P would argue that the general rule is that the party against whom the LCC doctrine is being applied must have the ability to avoid the accident, and only a small minority of cases take the view that LCC could still be applied where the defendant had lost his ability, due to his own negligence, and, in any event, P had not been negligent (as per the discussion of CN in P's negligence action against X).*

As to damages, the successful plaintiff would be entitled to recover for their past and future medical expenses, mental suffering (pain), and lost wages. Either P or S, if otherwise successful, could conceivably claim exemplary damages from X, which was liable for the rather gross conduct of its representative (the policeman) by the doctrine of *respondeat superior*. While many states permit members of an injured person's immediate family to sue the tortfeasor for loss of services and consortium, only a small minority of courts have held that such plaintiffs are entitled to sue for any resultant lack of *companionship*.

Finally, if any of the plaintiffs are successful against two defendants, each defendant would have contribution rights against the other.

The foregoing is a legitimate example of the application of a checklist to the problem-type examination question. So long as you perceive that the hypothetical involves negligence issues, you will automatically consider each of the essential doctrines (and the potential issues inherent herein) on the appropriate checklist. Once the issues are isolated, the test-taker can set forth the various arguments which each side to the controversy would make to persuade the court to resolve the issues in their favor.

---

* *Assumption of risk* would *not* be applicable to any of these actions because in none of them was the plaintiff knowledgeable of the hazardous circumstances (i.e. the malfunctioning traffic light which gave all motorists a "go" signal).

Another Example Demonstrating the Use of a Checklist on an Examination

The Parol Evidence Rule may come up in either Contracts' or Evidence. Basically, this doctrine states that where there is a writing which the parties have intended to be a complete and final expression of their agreement, prior oral or written evidence which varies or contradicts the express or implied terms of the writing will not be admissible. That the contract was intended to be the ultimate embodiment of the agreement between the parties is often proved by an "integration" or "merger" clause within the document. An example of this type of provision would be something like, "This contract constitutes the entire agreement between the parties hereto." The court (rather than the jury) determines whether an integration was intended, and usually from an examination of the face of the document only.

Under certain circumstances however, understandings which predate the signing of the writing may be admissible. For example, parol evidence is usually admissible to (i) explain any ambiguities, (ii) show that a condition precedent had to occur before the contract could become effective, (iii) to show that, as a result of fraud, duress, or a lack of consideration, the purported contract is not an enforceable obligation. Also, evidence of *collateral* oral agreements is ordinarily admissible to show terms which are not inconsistent with the writing and which the parties would not be expected to have included in the contract. Finally, subsequent oral or written agreements, whether they vary or contradict the prior contract, are not precluded by the

Parol Evidence Rule. The purpose of the Parol Evidence Rule is to permit parties to obtain certainty and finality as to the exact obligations which they are undertaking and benefits which they can expect to receive.

A checklist for the issues inherent in this doctrine might be the following:

Parol Evidence Rule

1. The writing must have been *intended* as an integration (final expression of the parties' agreements). Determined by court, usually from face of document.

2. Rule does not prevent pre-written contract evidence to

(a) Show fraud, duress, etc.

(b) Show failure of condition precedent to contract becoming effective, or performance of stated consideration.

(c) To explain ambiguities.

(d) To show *collateral* agreements—which are not contradictory and are the type which would not ordinarily be expected to be a part of the writing (UCC permits additional, consistent terms unless it's clear that writing was intended to be complete and exclusive manifestation of the agreement).

3. *Subsequent* oral or written agreements are always admissible.

A hypothetical pertaining to the Parol Evidence Rule, and a possible answer, will now be considered:

Mr. X was shown an apartment by Mr. Y, the building owner. X commented that he liked the place but the walls were a little faded. "Don't worry," Y said, "This apartment is due for a paint job very soon anyway." X responded, "In that case, I'll take it." Y then presented X with a contract entitled "Lease Agreement," the opening clause of which stated: "The following are the conditions upon which Y leases an apartment to X for one year." The agreement did not mention any duty upon Y to paint the premises.

Immediately after X signed the lease, he asked Y when the painting would begin. "In about three weeks," Y responded. Y then told X there would be a $25 cleaning fee, which X paid immediately. After repeated demands by X for two months, Y told X that due to inflation, none of the apartments would be painted for at least a year. X promptly moved out and Y sued him for the rent due under the balance of the lease term. X has retained you as his attorney, what advice would you give to him?

ANSWER

We must assume, of course, that Y will object to any attempt to introduce evidence of his promise to paint the apartment. A threshold issue would be whether the lease was intended to be an integration (i.e. final expression of parties agreements)? This issue is determined by the Court, and generally solely from the document itself. A minority of states do, however, permit resort to any relevant extrinsic evidence. Assuming this transaction arose in a jurisdiction which follows the majority rule, the writing does appear to represent an integration even though there is no ironclad clause to this effect (i.e. "There are no other agreements, oral or written, between the parties hereto".).

X could contend that the contract was obtained by fraud (the assurance that a paint job would be forthcoming), and that there was a failure of consideration since Y had promised to paint the premises. First, there is nothing in the facts to indicate Y deliberately misled X, and we will assume this could not be proved. Second, the *consideration* exception only permits one to show that the expressly promised consideration was not performed, *not* to show that there was an additional duty which the writing did not mention.

Next, X might argue that Y's promise to paint the apartment was a collateral agreement. However, such an agreement must (i) not contradict any term of the writing, and (ii) not be the type of understanding which is not ordinarily included within the contract. The promise to paint X's apartment would, Y would argue, be contrary to the opening paragraph of the lease which requires Y only to make an apartment available to X; although X could contend that said provision does not expressly exclude any other obligations on Y's part. Also, Y could argue that a duty to paint an apartment is certainly the type of obligation which would be found in a lease; although X could respond that an obligation to ameliorate an apartment is not usually contained in a form lease.

Finally, X might contend his inquiry as to when the paint job would commence and Y's answer *subsequent* to execution of the lease constituted a new agreement. Y would respond that this is a strained interpretation of that conversation, and it could not have been a new agreement since X gave no consideration for Y's promise. However, X might contend that his payment of the cleaning fee was the result of Y's representation that the premises would be painted in three weeks. Y would strenuously contend these obligations were not dependent upon each other and no intention to create a contract was present.

Based upon the foregoing, I would regretfully be obliged to inform X that the probabilities are that Y will prevail.

Another Example of a Checklist

One of the major areas of any Evidence course is the *Hearsay* doctrine. It results in the exclusion of certain type of statements and writings. There are numerous exceptions to this doctrine, however, and if one or more of these are present the communication in question will be admitted into evidence. These exceptions can be divided into two groups for purposes of recollection: those which will be permitted only where the declarant (the party who is responsible for the statement) is unavailable, and those where the availability of the declarant need not be shown to as a prerequisite to its admission into evidence. Thus, a party seeking to keep out of a certain piece of evidence will assert the hearsay doctrine; while the other side will argue (if at all possible) that one of the exceptions which permits admissibility nevertheless is present.

A slightly abbreviated checklist of Hearsay is shown below. Without undertaking an explanation of the terms and phrases mentioned thereon, it should suffice to demonstrate that the concepts previously described in this chapter for the construction of an effective checklist can be applied to virtually all law school courses. So long as a student recognizes that the test hypothetical contains a hearsay problem, the checklist will lead one to inquire **(1)** whether the hearsay doctrine is truly applicable at all, and **(2)** assuming it is, whether one or more of the possible exceptions are present. Of course, each term set forth on the checklist may be capable of spawning several sub-issues.

Hearsay

Hearsay—statement (writing or oral) made by someone (the declarant) other than the witness, to prove truth of matter stated

- (A) *Not hearsay*
    - (1) statement introduced other than to prove truth of matter stated:
        - (a) legal facts
        - (b) state of mind
    - (2) non-assertive conduct (minority rule)

Exceptions to hearsay doctrine

- (B) *Where declarant unavailable*
    - (1) *prior* testimony
    - (2) statement against *interest*
    - (3) *dying* declaration
- (C) *Whether declarant available or not*
    - (1) *business* records
    - (2) *admissions* by opponent
    - (3) statements for purpose of *medical* diagnosis and treatment
    - (4) *excited* utterances
    - (5) *present* mental, emotional or physical condition
    - (6) *official* records and reports
    - (7) *recorded* recollection

Summary

The essence of what has been described as the *checklist method* should be clear by this time. By (1) dividing a course into major areas, (2) organizing the important doctrines of each of these areas into the sequence in which the issues they embody are likely to arise on an examination, and (3) abbreviating this information so that it is easily re-created; you should be capable of reproducing an *effective* outline of an entire course in a few minutes. Therefore, provided you recognize the possible major areas contained in a particular test question, the applicability (or lack of same) of the issues inherent in the doctrines and principles of such areas will be considered in an orderly, methodical manner. Once the issues are spotted all the arguments which each side would assert should be discussed.

Other Preparation for Law School Exams

Beyond the Checklist

A law student should begin preparing for finals from the very first day of classes. Unless the reader is truly a genius, it will be impossible to cram a semester's work into a few weeks of intensive learning. The fatigue and grogginess which accompany *all-nighters* are usually incompatible with the analytical focus of a legal exam. Regardless of what your experience was at the undergraduate level, it would be sheer folly to leave preparation for law school finals to the last minute.

If you have been revising and memorizing your syntheses and checklists throughout the semester, most of your groundwork will have been completed well in advance of the exams. The balance of the necessary preparation is described on the following pages. Ideally, you should have completed the checklists for all your courses at least two full weeks prior to finals. This interim period should be solely for attendance of classes and review.

The Value of Class Attendance

A threshold question is probably, "Is it necessary to go

to classes?" The answer will usually be affirmative. My experience was that although classroom discussion rarely added much in the way of imparting new information, the lectures did enhance my understanding of the materials. Regardless of how carefully you have briefed the assigned cases, you cannot be certain of your proficiency in this area until your conclusions are confirmed by the discussion which ordinarily takes place at the lectures.

More important, however, is that the well-planned lecture will sharpen and improve a student's powers of legal analysis. The line of questioning presented by the professor will usually require a student to consider not only the parameters of each decision, but also the applicability (or lack of it) of the various principles of law to entirely different circumstances. Additional rationales and arguments, not mentioned in the opinions, are often brought out at the lectures. Also, some professors will utilize classes to summarize particular subjects, tie-together portions of the casebooks, and/or refer the student to informative Law Review articles.

In a somewhat lighter vein, there are other good reasons for attending classes. First, if you simply sat in the library and briefed cases all day, you would probably become a raving lunatic in about one month. Second, some classes are conducted in a way which is not only interesting, but downright humorous. The reader will thoroughly enjoy the manner in which a previously haughty student is humbled as a sarcastic professor punches numerous holes in the former's answers. Finally, if the reader is asked to join a study group, a normal consideration will be the intelligence of the other participants. The classroom discussion should give some indication of this attribute.

Effective Note-Taking

The type and extent of note-taking you do in law school will vary, depending upon the teaching style of each professor. However, in your first-year you will probably discover that, unlike your college experience, only a minority of professors will lecture. Law school classes are generally conducted in a manner which attempts to involve those in attendance. Some teachers will interrogate individual students about various aspects of the assigned reading, while others seem to perceive their role primarily as moderators and attempt to maximize input from the entire class.

The first rule of effective note-taking is to review the assigned cases immediately before class. Most professors will presume that everyone is familiar with the opinions which have been scheduled for discussion on that day, and therefore will not request those who are called upon to simply reiterate their briefs. Thus, unless you have a grasp of the materials upon which each class is grounded, you will probably have a difficult time understanding the ensuing discussions. Conversely, reviewing the assigned cases prior to classes will make it easier to follow the comments which are made, which in turn should make the class more interesting and meaningful.

Law students often seem to feel that it is essential to take several pages of notes for each lecture. This is probably a manifestation of the college psychosis that writing down everything the professor mentions is the correct thing to do. It is not necessary to be able to re-construct the entire period from your notes. Note-taking in law school should reflect your *understanding* of the comments made in the classroom, rather than your ability to take a modified type of shorthand. Thus, when the professor asks a question or poses a hypothetical it is important to grasp the principles of law or arguments which he seeks to demonstrate or elicit. *Understanding the thrust or purpose of a professor's remarks is usually more important than the answers which are given to them.*

Many professors begin their periods by asking a student to state the holding of one of the assigned cases. This often produces a discussion as to why or how the student's conclusion is deficient or too broad. Next, a description of the court's rationale will usually be required. This frequently leads to a discussion about the pros and cons of the court's reasoning. Very often the major consideration underlying the court's ruling may not have been enunciated in the opinion. The reader may find himself in disagreement with the court's decision in a surprisingly large number of instances as a consequence of the remarks made in class. It must be remembered, however, that inferior decisions are often the result of less than competent work by the attorneys who presented the case to the court.

The professor may then ask members of the class to distinguish, if possible, the opinion under scrutiny from one which had been discussed at an earlier date. *Distinguishing* one opinion from another means explaining why one court reached a result different from that of an earlier one, even though *similar* facts existed in each instance. For example, let us suppose that subsequent to *Katko* v. *Briney*, a trespasser (and potential burglar) suffered grievous injury when he attempted to scale an electrified fence (surrounding a factory) which had a large "Danger" sign posted on it. The trespasser sues the factory contending the rule of *Katko* v. *Briney* is controlling. The defendant-factory would attempt to distinguish the latter decision by pointing out that (1) a factory rather than a vacant summer home is involved, and (2) a warning had been given. Plaintiff's response, of course, would be that (1) the factual differences noted by the defendant are not persuasive in view of the overriding rationale of *Katko* v. *Briney*, and (2) a sign marked "Danger" could be interpreted as referring to the type of work being undertaken in the factory. The ability to distinguish cases is important for the preparation of effective syntheses and discussing issues in a superior manner.

Hopefully, the professor will then offer a hypothetical problem and challenge the class to explain how and why (or why not) the outcome would change as new facts are added or subtracted. This is probably the most stimulating aspect of any class. It obliges you to ask yourself how each new circumstance might cause the court to rule in favor of one side rather than the other. A slight twist in the given facts might bring entirely new legal and policy considerations into play. The ability to recognize the potential issues and arguments which would arise as the circumstances of a hypothetical are altered is a valid indicator of the development of your legal mind.

Finally, it is important for you to be highly discriminating in your note-taking at all times. It should be borne in mind that the greater the number of pages of classnotes taken, the more difficult it will be to merge this information into the syntheses. As noted earlier, it is usually more important to have grasped *why* particular questions were asked, rather than how they were answered. If you are concentrating on writing down every word said in the classroom, the main purpose of the professor's line of questioning may be lost. If a point or argument is made which you consider valuable for further use, then by all means it should be jotted down. Usually, however, only the thrust or main point of a particular discussion need be preserved for future review.

Study Groups

To compare notes and verify their understanding of the materials, several students will sometimes agree to meet at prearranged times. Provided the members of your study group are conscientious and things proceed in a business-like manner, these gatherings can be helpful. However, if the members are not fully prepared, or if the meetings become disorganized or deteriorate into discussions about personal or social matters, valuable time will be lost. It is suggested that if this procedure is adopted, the number of participants should be limited to no more than four, and there be a definite understanding at the very beginning that frivolity will not be accepted. The number of such meetings should usually be limited to no more than twice a month.

In the motion picture entitled *The Paper Chase*, the study group of which the hero is a member decides that each person will create the synthesis for a particular subject. This should *never* be done. First, there is the possibility that one or more of the participants will drop out, become ill or otherwise fail to complete his assignment. Even if this does not occur, it may ultimately turn out that the member of the study group responsible for an important course is at the very bottom of the class, and actually did a very poor job on his particular synthesis. Most important, however, is the fact that synthesizing is absolutely essential to a genuine understanding of the interrelationship of the various course materials, which is crucial for success on hypothetical-type exams. Under no circumstances should you attempt to avoid the *hard* thinking inherent in the creation of a good synthesis by permitting another to perform this task.

Supplemental Study Materials: Outlines, Hornbooks and Restatements

At some point in your law school career, you will undoubtedly be exposed to published outlines, hornbooks, or Restatements. The major difference between these works and casebooks is that the former do not contain actual opinions. They do ordinarily state the general principles and rules which comprise a particular field of law, and are thus often referred to as sources of *black-letter* law. The general principles and rules in hornbooks and Restatements (and sometimes outlines) are usually followed by examples and a discussion of the basic policies which underlie the propositions of law. Outlines and hornbooks are one-volume works; Restatements often comprise multiple volumes and frequently contain hypotheticals which illustrate the various propositions of law which have been enunciated. Restatements and hornbooks can be found in most law school libraries; they have usually been written by law professors whose areas of expertise are in the particular subjects treated. It is probably a good idea for you to familiarize yourself with these works at the inception of a semester.

Probably the best way of discussing these works in a meaningful manner is to give some examples, and then comment upon their pros and cons. One of the topics which will be encountered in a Torts course is battery. The fol-

lowing description of this subject is contained in a horn-
book entitled *The Law of Torts.**

BATTERY

The interest in freedom [sic] from intentional and
unpermitted contacts with the plaintiff's person is protected by an action for the tort commonly called battery. The protection extends to any part of the body,
or to anything which is attached to it and practically
identified with it. Thus contact with the plaintiff's
clothing, or with a cane, a paper, or any other object
held in his hand, will be sufficient; and the same is true
of the chair in which he sits, the horse or the car which
he is riding or driving, or the person against whom he
is leaning. His interest in the integrity of his person
includes all those things which are in contact or connected with it.

Since the disappearance of the distinction between
trespass and case, it is no longer important that the
contact is not brought about by a direct application of
force such as a blow, and it is enough that the defendant sets a force in motion which ultimately produces
the result, as by setting out food for the plaintiff to eat
which contains a poison, or digging a pitfall in the path
on which he is to walk. It is not essential that the plaintiff should be conscious of the contact at the time it
occurs. Interest in personal integrity still is entitled to
protection, although the plaintiff is asleep or under an
anaesthetic, or otherwise unaware of what is going on.
The invasion is equally great; and the girl who is
kissed in her sleep is likely to be affronted quite as
much, and perhaps more, when she discovers it after

* W. L. Prosser, *The Law of Torts*, 4th Ed. (West Publishing Co.,
1971).

the event, as when she knows it at the time. Proof of the technical invasion of the integrity of the plaintiff's person by even an entirely harmless, but offensive, contact entitles him to vindication of his legal right by an award of nominal damages, and the establishment of the tort cause of action entitles him also to compensation for the mental disturbance inflicted upon him, such as fright or humiliation. The defendant's liability for the harm resulting from his conduct extends, as in most other cases of intentional torts, to consequences which he did not intend, and could not reasonably have foreseen, upon the obvious basis that it is better for unexpected losses to fall upon the intentional wrongdoer than upon the innocent victim. Since battery usually is a matter of the worst kind of intentions, it is a tort which frequently justifies punitive damages; but in the comparatively infrequent case where the defendant has acted in good faith under a mistake of fact, but still has committed the tort, punitive damages are not allowed.

Character of Defendant's Act

In order to be liable for battery, the defendant must have done some positive and affirmative act; mere passive obstruction of the plaintiff's passage, while it may perhaps constitute another tort, does not amount to a battery. The act must cause, and must be intended to cause, an unpermitted contact. Mere negligence, or even recklessness, which creates only a risk that the contact will result, may afford a distinct cause of action in itself, but under modern usage of the term it is not enough for battery.

The original purpose of the courts in providing the action for battery undoubtedly was to keep the peace by affording a substitute for private retribution. The element of personal indignity involved always has been given considerable weight. Consequently, the defendant is liable not only for contacts which do actual physical harm, but also for those relatively trivial ones which are merely offensive and insulting. Spitting in the face is a battery, as is forcibly removing the plaintiff's hat, or any other contact brought about in a rude and insolent manner. "The least touching of another in anger," said Chief Justice Holt, "is a battery"; and no harm or actual damage of any kind is required. The plaintiff is entitled to demand that the defendant keep his hands to himself although the contact results in no visible injury.

The gist of the action for battery is not the hostile intent of the defendant, but rather the absence of consent to the contact on the part of the plaintiff.

The defendant may be liable where he has intended only a joke, or even a compliment as where an unappreciative woman is kissed without her consent, or a misguided effort is made to render assistance. The plaintiff is entitled to protection according to the usages of decent society, and hostile contacts, or those which are contrary to all good manners, need not be tolerated. At the same time, in a crowded world, a certain amount of personal contact is inevitable, and must be accepted. Consent is assumed to all those ordinary contacts which are customary and reasonably necessary to the common intercourse of life, such as a tap on the shoulder to attract attention, a friendly grasp of the arm, or a casual jostling to make a passage. There is as yet no very satisfactory authority as to whether even such innocuous and generally permitted contacts can become tortious if they are inflicted with knowledge that the individual plaintiff objects to them and refuses to permit them. Although where there is any doubt at all the plaintiff's expressed wishes may very well turn the scale as to what is reasonable, it may be questioned whether any individual can be permitted, by his own fiat, to erect a glass cage around himself, and to announce that all physical contact with his person is at the expense of liability.

The time and place, and the circumstances under which the act is done, will necessarily affect its unpermitted character, and so will the relations between the parties. A stranger is not to be expected to tolerate liberties which would be allowed by an intimate friend. But unless the defendant has special reason to believe that more or less will be permitted by the individual plaintiff, the test is what would be offensive to an ordinary person not unduly sensitive as to his dignity. The intent required is only the intent to bring about such a contact; and given that, liability will depend upon whether there is a privilege, because of the plaintiff's individual consent, or otherwise.

Another discussion of battery is found in an outline entitled *Torts*.*

I. INTENTIONAL TORTS
A. TORTS TO THE PERSON
1. Battery
Prima facie case: <u>Act by Defendant</u>
<u>Intent</u>
<u>Harmful or Offensive Touch-</u>
<u>ing</u>
<u>Causation</u>

---

* W. A. Rutter, *Torts* 10th Ed. (Gilbert Law Summaries, 1974).

(Lack of Consent—discussed
as a Defense, infra)

a. **Act by defendant:** The word "act" as used in
intentional torts means an external manifestation of the actor's will; it refers to some volitional movement by the actor of some part of
his body. Thus, if D intentionally drove his
automobile into P, the "act" complained of
would not be the driving of the automobile,
but rather the movement by D of his arms
and legs in setting the automobile into motion
and directing it at P. [Restatement, Torts 2d
§ 2]

   (1) **Unconscious acts:** Because of the requirement of a "volitional" movement, the
   movements of epileptics, persons asleep
   or under the influence of drugs, are not
   generally sufficient "acts" for the purpose
   of establishing liability for intentional
   torts. [Lobert v. Pack, 9 A.2d 365]

   (2) **Reflex actions:** On the other hand, a muscular reaction by a person in command of
   his senses is always an "act" unless it is
   purely a reflex action in which the mind
   and will have no share. Thus, the blinking
   of eyelids in defense against an approaching missile is not an "act" because it is
   purely reflexive. But, if D, finding himself about to fall, stretches his hand out
   to save himself, the stretching out of his
   hand is an "act" . . . his mind has grasped
   the situation and dictated a muscular con-
   traction in an effort to prevent the fall,

[c f, Filippone v. Reisenburger, 119 N.Y.S. 632]

(3) **Incompetents:** Persons who are not legally competent are still capable of volitional conduct; i.e., insane persons or minors may be held liable for their acts. [McGuire v. Almy, 8 N.E.2d 760]

b. **Intent:** The "act" done by D must have been done with the intent to inflict a harmful or an offensive touching on P or a third person, or to put P or a third person in apprehension of an immediate harmful or offensive touching, I.e., he must have acted for the purpose of causing such result. [Rest.2d § 13(a)]

(1) **Test:** Whether D had the requisite intent is measured by the "substantial certainty test"—D must have known or have been substantially certain that a harmful or offensive touching would result from his act. [Lambrecht v. Schreyer, 152 N.W. 645]

(a) **Example:** Being late for an appointment, D decides to push his way through a crowd, causing P to lose his balance and strike his head on the sidewalk. D is liable for P's injuries, even though he had no actual desire to injure P. It is enough that D acted with a substantial certainty that his acts would cause a bodily contact with the crowd, of which P was a member, and that P's injuries resulted therefrom. [See Baldinger v. Banks, 201 N.Y.S.2d 629]

(2) **Motives immaterial:** The same distinction must be drawn between "malice" and "intent" as is drawn in criminal law. (See Criminal Law Summary) "Malice" refers to D's motives, and motives are generally immaterial. We are concerned here only with whether the act was wilfully done . . . i.e., whether D had the requisite intent under the substantial certainty test, above.

   (a) However, if "malice" (intent to injure) exists, D may be held liable for punitive damages (see below).

(3) **Transfer of intent doctrine:** A mistake as to identity of the victim does not negate intent. It is sufficient to impose liability on D that the harmful result which he intended to inflict on X actually is inflicted on P, even though this was not what D actually intended. The courts will "transfer" his wrongful intent from the intended victim to the actual victim, to hold D liable. [Rest.2d § 16]

   (a) **Example:** D sees his best friend, P, talking to D's enemy, X. D throws a stone at X which misses him but which strikes P, putting out his eye. D is liable to P for battery; his wrongful intent to inflict a harmful touching on X is "transferred" to P, even though this is clearly not what D actually desired. [Carnes v. Thompson, 48 S.W.2d 903]

   (b) **Assault vs. battery:** The transfer of

intent doctrine can also be used to establish liability for a battery even though D's intent was only to inflict an assault, or vice versa.

   1) For example, suppose D intended only to frighten X by throwing the stone at him. His intent to put X in apprehension of an immediate harmful touching (an assault) is sufficient to establish D's liability to P for battery.

   2) Or, suppose D actually intended to hit X with the stone, but missed both X and P, although P was put in apprehension of an immediate harmful touching. D's intent to inflict an actual touching on X (a battery) is sufficient to establish his liability to P for assault.

c. **Harmful or offensive touching:** D's intentional act must have resulted in the infliction of a harmful or offensive touch of P's person, or something so closely associated with P as to make the touching tantamount to a physical invasion of P's person. There must, however, be an actual touching; "coming close" is not enough to constitute a battery.

   (1) **"Harmful" touching:** A touching is "harmful" if it inflicts any pain, injury, disfigurement or impairment of any bodily organ or function.

   (2) **"Offensive" touching:** Any touching of P, or something "closely associated with his person" which would offend a reasonable

person's sense of personal dignity, is regarded as an "offensive" touching.

(a) Things "closely associated with the plaintiff's person" cover the situations where D knocks P's hat off his head; or strikes the dog which P is leading on a leash; or the camera which P is operating; or grabs a plate out of his hand. [Fisher v. Carrousel Motor Hotel, Inc., 424 S.W.2d 627; Rest.2d § 18]

(b) A touching at which a reasonable person would not take offense, but at which P does take offense, is not sufficient to impose liability. [Rest. 2d § 19]

(3) **Plaintiff unaware of touching:** P need not have knowledge of the touching at the time thereof. Thus, if D kisses P while the latter is asleep, but does not waken or harm her, the kiss may be a sufficiently "offensive" touching to establish liability even though P only learned of the contact later. [Rest.2d §19, comment "d"]

d. **Causation—substantial factor test:** The harmful or offensive touching must be legally caused by the defendant's act or some force set in motion thereby. The causation requirement is satisfied if the defendant's conduct is a "substantial factor" in bringing about the injury, and the injury is of the type he intended to inflict. [Garratt v. Dailey, 304 P.2d 681—D pulled chair out from under P who was about to sit down; Rest. § 870, comment "f"]

(1) **Example:** D throws a stone at P, intending to injure him. The stone misses its mark, but strikes a pile of rocks, setting loose an avalanche which kills P. D's act was a "substantial factor" in bringing about the injuries which led to P's death (it set loose the avalanche which caused the injuries). D is, therefore, liable for P's death.

(2) **Example:** D digs a trap along a footpath which he knows P habitually uses, with intent to injure P. D is liable for any injuries sustained by P (or any third person) falling in the trap. Rationale: D's acts set in motion the forces which actually inflicted injuries of the type intended, and hence were a "substantial factor" in bringing about those injuries.

(3) **No liability for external causes:** However, where the harm to P was actually caused by some outside force, and D's conduct was not a "substantial factor" in activating this outside force, D is not liable. Rationale: There is not sufficient assurance that P wouldn't have been injured anyhow. [Rest.2d § 435A]

    (a) **Example:** D chases P with the intent to strike him. As he is fleeing, P is struck by lightning. D is not liable for P's injuries. The fact that P wouldn't have been where he was (and hence wouldn't have been injured) but for being chased by D, isn't enough. D's conduct was not a "substantial factor" in causing the lightning.

(4) **Compare—negligence liability:** The law holds an intentional wrongdoer liable for all of the consequences of his acts, whether or not foreseeable. However, in negligence cases, causation operates to cut off liability at an earlier point . . . so that a negligent tortfeasor may well be excused from liability as to injuries for which an intentional tortfeasor would be liable (see infra, p. 39).

e. **Damages:** The tort is complete upon the commission of the harmful or offensive touching. The court will award damages in such amount as it deems reasonable to compensate for the touching ("general" damages). No other special damage need be shown.

(1) **Special damages:** However, if D's touching has actually caused "special damages" to P—physical disability, medical expenses, emotional distress, etc.—these may also be recovered.

(2) **Punitive damages:** Further, wherever it appears that D's act was motivated by an intention to injure or harm P, the court may, in addition, award punitive ("exemplary") damages against D.

Still another explanation of battery is contained in the **Restatement of the Law, Torts 2d.*** The actual description was slightly lengthier, but the following will suffice.

---

* Adopted and promulgated by the American Law Institute (American Law Institute Publishers, 1965).

§ 13. Battery: Harmful Contact

An actor is subject to liability to another for battery if

(a) he acts intending to cause a harmful or offensive contact with the person of the other or a third person, or an imminent apprehension of such a contact, and

(b) a harmful contact with the person of the other directly or indirectly results.

Comment:

a. At common law the appropriate form of action for bodily harm directly resulting from an act done with the intention stated in Clause (a) was trespass for battery. (See Scope Note to this Topic.)

b. As to the meaning of the word "act," see § 2. As to the necessity of an act, see § 14.

c. As to the meaning of "intending," see § 8 A. If an act is done with the intention described in this Section, it is immaterial that the actor is not inspired by any personal hostility to the other, or a desire to injure him. Thus the fact that the defendant who intentionally inflicts bodily harm upon another does so as a practical joke, does not render him immune from liability so long as the other has not consented. This is true although the actor erroneously believes that the other will regard it as a joke, or that the other has, in fact, consented to it. One who plays dangerous practical jokes on others takes the risk that his victims may not appreciate the humor of his conduct and may not take it in good part. So too, a surgeon who performs an operation upon a patient who has refused to submit to it is not relieved from liability by the fact that he honestly and, indeed, justifiably believes that the operation is necessary to save the patient's life. Indeed, the fact that medical testimony shows that the patient would have died had the operation not been performed and that the operation has effected a complete cure is not enough to relieve the physician from liability. See § 892 A, Illustration 2.

d. As to the meaning of "subject to liability," see § 5. The defendant's act must be a legal cause of the contact with the plaintiff's person, and the liability is defeated by any privilege available to the defendant under §§ 49–156. In particular, the plaintiff's consent to the contact with his person will prevent the liability. The absence of such consent is inherent in the very idea of those invasions of interests of personality which, at common law, were the subject of an action of trespass for battery, assault, or false imprisonment. Therefore the absence of consent is a matter essential to the cause of action, and it is uniformly held that it must be proved by the plaintiff as a necessary part of his case. The effect of consent is covered in §§ 892–892 D.

§ 14. Necessity of Act by Defendant

To make the actor liable for a battery, the harmful bodily contact must be caused by an act done by the person whose liability is in question.

Comment:

a. This Section is an application of the general rule stated in § 13.

b. The word "act" is used in the Restatement of this Subject to denote an exertion of the will manifested in the external world. (See § 2.) Thus, a muscular movement which is purely reflexive or the convulsive movements of an epileptic are not acts in the sense in which that word is used in the Restatement. So too, movements of the body during sleep or while the will is otherwise in abeyance are not acts. An external manifestation of the will is necessary to constitute an act, and an act is necessary to make one liable under the rule stated in § 13. Therefore, it is not enough to make one liable that some third person has utilized a part of his body as an instrument by which to carry out the third person's intention to cause harm to another. In such a case, the third person is the actor.

Illustration:

1. A pushes B against C, knocking C down and breaking his leg. A, and not B, is subject to liability to C.

c. There is perhaps no essential reason why, under the modern law, liability for battery might not be based on inaction, where it is intended to result and does result in a harmful or offensive contact with the person. Apparently, however, no such case has arisen, and what little authority there is denies the liability.

Illustration:

2. A, a member of a Caledonian Society, seeks to enter a room in which the Society is meeting. B, a police officer, obstructed A's entrance by standing motionless in the doorway. Bodily contact results from the acts of A, and not B. B is not liable to A for battery.

§ 15. What Constitutes Bodily Harm
Bodily harm is any physical impairment of the condition of another's body, or physical pain or illness.

Comment:

a. There is an impairment of the physical condition of another's body if the structure or function of any part of the other's body is altered to any extent even though the alteration causes no other harm. A contact

which causes no bodily harm may be actionable as a
violation of the right to freedom from the intentional
infliction of offensive bodily contacts. (See §§ 18–20.)
Illustration:

1. A has a wart on his neck. His physician, B,
advises him to submit to an operation for its removal.
A refuses to do so. Later A consents to another
operation, and for that purpose is anesthetized. B
removes the wart. The removal in no way affects A's
health, and is in fact beneficial. A has suffered bodily
harm.

b. The minute disturbance of the nerve centers
caused by fear, shock or other emotions does not constitute bodily harm. It may, however, result in some
appreciable illness or have some other effect upon the
physical condition of the body which constitutes bodily
harm.

Illustration:

2. A drives his automobile close to the curb for the
purpose of frightening B, a pedestrian. B is put in
fear of his bodily safety but is otherwise unharmed.
B has not sustained bodily harm.

First, a discussion of the negative side of the ledger. The
quality of outlines and hornbooks varies greatly. Some are
infinitely more well-organized and concise than others.
These general works may not reflect the special importance
which your professor has given to a particular topic. Conversely, they may devote more detail than is necessary to
particular aspects of a course. Of course, a substantial
amount of time will be consumed (especially in the case of
Restatements and hornbooks) in reading and taking notes
on these materials. In doing any type of non-assigned work,

a law student must carefully weigh the hours spent and the benefits received.

Significantly, these works usually fail to emphasize the interrelationship of the various topics and doctrines of a particular course. The format of hornbooks and outlines often parallels the table of contents of the corresponding casebook. As noted in the chapter on Synthesizing, such a format is often inconsistent with the creation of an effective synthesis. Also, although these books usually contain examples of a particular rule or principle, such illustrations cannot take the place of actually *understanding* them. For example, when studying for the California Bar I reduced the topic of battery to six words—"An intentional non-privileged contact upon another."* Such a terse summary is possible only after you have truly grasped the essence of a particular concept.

Restatements, hornbooks and outlines have two other flaws. First, since their primary emphasis is upon rules and principles they do not give the reader a feeling for the interaction between legal principles and facts which occurs when a case is argued before a court. Only actual opinions can give you the flavor of this process. Secondly, as mentioned earlier, the capacity to extract and interpret the principle of law represented by a written opinion is crucial to the study of law. A student who attempts to avoid this task may be doing himself an irreparable disservice.

On the positive side, Restatements, hornbooks and outlines can assist and further your legal education in several ways. First, these works can often be very helpful in articulating or formulating the propositions of law contained

---

* It was unnecessary to go into concepts such as transferred intent or damages because these are inherent in any intentional tort upon another person.

in the casebook opinions. Hornbooks and outlines may permit you to obtain an overview of a topic or doctrine in a relatively short period of time, which in turn may result in the creation of more effective syntheses. In some instances, outlines and hornbooks serve as a good means of verifying the completeness of your syntheses. These works are probably, however, most important when you are unable to understand a certain doctrine or feel lost in a particular subject. Since you may be unable to obtain the type of individual instruction required from a professor, you may find that hornbooks are often the best (if not the exclusive) means of filling blindspots in your understanding. Finally, the hypothetical examples contained in Restatements are in my opinion especially useful learning tools.

In summary, Restatements, hornbooks and outlines should in no event be permitted to supplant the assigned materials. Although you must be knowledgeable of the basic legal principles and rules which comprise a particular body of law, it is also crucial for you to develop the ability to be able to state the holding of a decision and argue for its applicability (or inapplicability) to a somewhat different set of facts. On the other hand, if you are having difficulty in getting the handle on a particular subject or concept, or have sufficient free time, then by all means you should consult these works. If you perform *all* of the steps, including the mental exercises, suggested in the previous chapters you will have little need of outside reading.

It is probably appropriate to mention a word or so about *canned briefs* at this juncture. These works are barely worth the paper they are written on. First, the summaries found in these books contain precisely the same flaws as the conventional briefs described earlier. Second, they also often omit significant dictum and the commentary which follows opinions contained in the casebook. Most significant, however, is the fact that canned briefs impede the development of your ability to read and extract legal principles from written decisions—a skill which is crucial to the competent attorney.

Useful Memorization Techniques

This book has properly stressed that the focus of law school study must be upon understanding and analysis, rather than memorization. Nevertheless, it will be necessary to remember the modicum of legal principles contained on each of the checklists. Although you have probably developed your own method of recalling large masses of information in college, the following techniques might prove helpful.

Mnemonics are techniques which facilitate the recollection of data. Of course, mnemonic devices need not make sense. Any variety of words or syllables which assists the memory process is valid. At this time, please refer to the negligence checklist found in the preceding chapter. To remember the skeleton of this checklist, I devised the terms SPAD-FDD-WHO (pronounced "spad-fed-who"). The S stands for *Standard,* the P for *Proof,* the A for *Actual Causation,* the D for *Duty,* the latter D for *Defenses,* and the WHO for "Who is liable, for what?" An abbreviation for the potential sub-issues under damages could be HAPEC (*Hit, Avoidable* Consequences, *Past*-Future, *Exemplary* and *Companionship*).

While studying for the California Bar I devised a checklist of possible grounds for defending against a breach of contract action. This is an entirely different problem area from that described in the previous chapter of this book. That portion dealt with the agreement-acceptance process (i.e. was a contract formed?). Questions about the defenses referred to below arise only after the requisite elements of an agreement are present. An easy-to-remember checklist of fourteen potential defenses could be SUMANIR-WE-NARC:

S = Statute of frauds
U = Unconscionable or adhesion provisions
M = Material breach by other side
A = Anticipatory breach by other side
N = Narrow construction (interpretation)
 I = Impossibility of performance
R = Rescission
W = Waiver
E = Estoppel
N = Novation
A = Accord and satisfaction
R = Release
C = Cancellation

Of course, each of the doctrines mentioned above might warrant its own checklist.*

The major areas of Torts law could be reduced to PINS-DMP (pronounced "pins-damp"): P = *Products liability,* I = *Intentional* torts to person and/or property, N = *Negligence,* S = *Strict liability,* D = *Defamation,* M = *Misrepresentation,* and P = *Privacy.* Three terms which might aid recollection of the Hearsay synthesis could be NUR-PID-BAMEPOR. NUR stands for words *Not, Unavailable,* and

---

* The foregoing list of prospective defenses to liability on a contracts' action is not exhaustive. There are others such as fraud, duress, illegality, etc., but these were not included on the syntheses because there was little likelihood they would appear on the exam, or would be blatantly obvious if they did.

Regardless, the key words for the three subsections; P = *Prior* testimony, I = statement against *interest*, D = *Death*, B = *Business* records, etc. Any combination of letters or words which helps you to recall the important doctrines is valid.

It is sometimes said that utilization of mnemonics is dangerous; that is, if the mnemonic is forgotten, so would be all of the principles and doctrines that it represented. There is a story of an apparently brilliant law student who reduces all his notes to a single page; then to a single paragraph, and finally to a solitary word. Despite this feat, the student did poorly on his exam. When questioned as to how this could have occurred since the entire course had been distilled down to a single word, our hero replied, "I forgot the word." Nevertheless, the dispositive answer to this argument is that even if you totally forget a mnemonic, you are still in no worse situation than you would have been if a memorization device had never been employed.

One of my fellow students at Columbia once remarked to me that utilizing a recorder was another good means of remembering important information. This person had purchased a cassette, dictated his syntheses on to blank tapes and then played them back whenever performing relatively thoughtless tasks (i.e. dressing, brushing teeth, etc.). He stated to me that in this manner he was able to absorb important doctrines into his subconscious. Although this person received no small amount of kidding about the way a strange voice was constantly heard emanating from his room, he probably enjoyed the last laugh. He was a member of the Law Review, clerked for an appellate court justice in New York and is presently associated with a prestigious law firm in Los Angeles.

A final recollection technique which this writer found beneficial was to go over in his mind the potential issues and sub-issues inherent in each topic or doctrine for about one-half hour immediately before going to sleep. I have read that the mind is highly susceptible to new ideas during this interval. Of course, if your powers of concentration are adequately developed, any free moments (i.e., waiting for a bus, walking to and from your residence, etc.) can be utilized to go over the syntheses and checklists. Regardless of what techniques you ultimately employ, when in law school—THINK LAW!

A Working Knowledge of Legal Research

Although it does not pertain directly to studying for law school exams, a word or two about legal research is in order at this juncture. You should not leave law school until you have at least a working knowledge of how to look up *all* of the pertinent law on a particular topic. Unfortunately, many law schools will give a lecture and distribute materials on this subject at the commencement of your legal education, and then almost never require the students to refer to them again. With the possible exception of Moot Court, few courses will compel you to seek out definitive answers to specific questions. The result is that the average law student never learns or soon forgets the most basic research skills.

If you have the opportunity to *clerk* for a law firm* or judge, probably the very first thing you will be requested to do is write a memorandum on a particular point of law. You will not be able to perform this task with proficiency unless and until you know how to utilize all of the follow-

---

* Many firms hire students for the summer between the second and third academic years.

ing: (1) the various state and federal reporters (and especially the key-number system devised by the West Publishing Company for finding propositions of law for each subject), (2) secondary materials such as digests, encyclopedias (i.e. Corpus Juris Secumdum, American Jurisprudence), *American Law Reports* (sometimes called the ALR), treatises and law review articles, (3) the various annotated state and federal enactments and administrative regulations, and (4) *both* case law and statutes. A law student should also be aware of how to trace the legislative history of a particular provision. Finally, the Commerce Clearing House (CCH) provides a biweekly loose-leaf service in many areas of federal law (bankruptcy, corporations, taxation, etc.), which you should know how to use. You should ask the professor of each course what sources he or she would utilize in researching a particular problem in his or her area, and then familiarize yourself with such works.

Once the requisite knowledge of the basic sources and how to utilize them is acquired, the key to effective research is simply tenacity. Unless there is a Supreme Court decision exactly on point,* you should review every work which could possibly shed light upon the issue under study. Treatises are often helpful in this context because they permit the reader to obtain an overview of the entire topic and may disclose policy considerations which were not otherwise evident. If you discover new issues or sub-issues which the person who is assigned the project did not mention, you should also research and discuss them. When all the pertinent information is finally assembled, the authorities should be arranged and discussed in the order of their persuasiveness (i.e. statutes, cases, treatises, Restatements, and articles).

* A statute may appear to be conclusive of an issue, but may have been interpreted in a conflicting manner.

In summary, knowing where and how to research the applicable law is an integral part of your legal education. The degree of expertise demonstrated in this area could well be the determining factor in obtaining the employment you desire. You should ascertain the basic research tools of each subject, and acquire at least a working knowledge of them before graduating from law school.

The Importance of Reviewing Prior Examinations

A. *Why Analyzing Old Exams Is Very Important*

It is extremely important to review as many old exams as possible. As noted in the introductory chapter, the transition from synthesis to finals can literally be a shocking experience if you have never seen a hypothetical-type exam before. Most law schools have on file in the library the tests which were given in a particular course for the last two to four academic years. If the institution which you attend does not, it is well worth the time and trouble to make a special trip to a law school which does make exams from prior years available. It is strongly suggested that you make a copy of every old exam you can obtain at the beginning of the semester, since the demand for these documents frequently increases as finals time draws closer.

The old exams for each course should be scrutinized periodically throughout the semester. Preferably after each chapter, but in no event less frequently than after the synthesis of each major area is completed. Generally, the chronological order of exam questions will follow the sequence of the materials contained in the casebook. Thus, for example, the first hypothetical on a law school test will often involve the initial three chapters of the casebook, the second question may pertain to chapters four through eight, etc. There are several reasons why reviewing exams from past years facilitates academic success.

First, analyzing old exams should give you a greater understanding of the manner in which the rules and principles found on your synthesis becomes issues on the finals. If you have been devising hypotheticals for all of the synthesized material as each chapter and subdivision is completed, you will probably have already acquired a good grasp of this transformation. Nevertheless, there is no substitute for the real thing. Where, for example, you recognize that a contracts question involves an offer-acceptance problem, you should carefully consider the potential applicability of each issue on your synthesis to the hypothetical.

Perceiving the context in which issues have arisen on past finals may pursuade you to modify your syntheses to more accurately reflect the sequence in which the issues are likely to arise. Also, as the low probability or obviousness of certain doctrines or topics becomes apparent you may decide that such information may safely be dropped from your checklists. Illustrations of this phenomenon in Contracts' are topics such as adhesion agreements, illegality, lack of capacity (i.e. proper age) and those situations where neither side intends promises to have legal consequences. Thus, prior exams help you to anticipate the issues, and should therefore be examined throughout the school year.

Exams from prior years should also reveal which causes of action or topics tend to be included in the same hypothetical. For example, a review of Torts exams may indicate that legal controversies involving assault, battery, false imprisonment and defenses to intentional interference with person and property often appear in one question; while issues pertaining to defamation, invasion of privacy and intentional infliction of emotional distress appear in another. Similarly, offer, termination, acceptance and damages problems are often contained in the first hypothetical of a Contracts' final; and parol evidence, interpretation or statute of frauds issues in a later one. By seeing at firsthand which types of legal problems have a tendency to appear together, you will minimize the likelihood of overlooking these areas.

You will also probably discover that although a surprisingly high number of major areas are covered in an exam, each one usually appears only once. Thus, if you perceive the same issue in two different hypotheticals, a closer look would be warranted. Finally, understanding how a particular phrase or sentence of the question fitted into previous answers will help you to recognize the relevance of similar information if it appears on your final.

To get an idea of actual law school exams, see the Appendix, pages 179 through 251.

B. *Ways to Verify Your Answer*

You should take the time to write out at least one exam for each course to determine if there will be any difficulty in staying within the prescribed time limitations. The other finals should be outlined in detail. You should go over your answer several times throughout the semester, preferably at least a few weeks apart so that a fresh perspective can be brought to bear upon the problem. My experience was that new issues and arguments were almost always discovered, even though the question was being analyzed for the second or third time. Of course, if you wait until the semester is almost over to undertake this task periodic review will be impossible.

There are several means you can utilize to evaluate your ability to isolate and discuss all of the issues contained within the test hypotheticals. One is to ask the professor of each course to permit you to check your answer against the paper of a student who received an A for that year's exam. Many law schools require graders to retain examination answers for at least one year. If your teacher has prepared a model answer or outline, ask to see it. One of my professors initially expressed astonishment when I made such a request, but permitted me to borrow it a short time afterwards and even commended me for my aggressive attitude. Don't be too shy or embarrassed to ask your professors for assistance at any stage of the semester. Furthering students' understanding of their subject is, after all, precisely why they are being paid.

Another way of checking your answers is to ask an upperclassman to go over them with you. At Columbia, each freshman was assigned an advisor to help him or her with any questions pertaining to legal study. If your school does not have such a person, you could ask someone on Law Review or someone who received a high grade in the particular subject in which you desire assistance to review and comment upon your written answers. If necessary, serious consideration should be given to paying such a person for his time. Such a relatively small investment could yield excellent returns.

Yet another way to confirm your proficiency at isolating and discussing the issues on prior finals is to get together with a small group of students who have reviewed the same exams to compare answers. Of course, the quality of these meetings will often be a direct function of the legal acumen of the participants. If this method is selected, it would be wise to require each member of the group to draft his or her own hypotheticals with the objective of including as many issues as possible. Such an exercise should enhance the creators' understanding of the manner in which principles and rules of law subsequently spawn issues.

In summary, the importance of outlining the issues and supporting arguments contained on past examinations is difficult to overemphasize. The fact that you may have created magnificent syntheses and checklists will mean little if you are unable to apply this information to the hypotheticals which appear on the final. As noted in the beginning pages, there is a vast difference between reading opinions in which the issues are clearly defined, and spotting and discussing those issues in the context of an alien, complex, factual situation. Analysis at regular intervals throughout the semester of tests which were given in prior years should greatly facilitate this crucial transition.

Guidelines for Writing Law School Exams

Basics—the Physical Details

First, try to get a reasonable amount of hours of sleep the evening before the examination. Drowsiness is not conducive to perceptive thinking. The customary rules of test-taking should be observed; arrive on time, with a watch, and with an appropriate number of writing utensils; usually scratch-paper of some type will be passed out before the test booklet is distributed. This interval can be utilized to recreate the checklists on the scratch sheets if the professor has not permitted notes to be taken into the exam room.* If the checklists are not completed when the test begins, take a minute or two to complete them *before* beginning the examination. If any item is forgotten, finish the rest of the outline and then begin the examination—the missing datum will usually be recalled in a short while.

Many law schools will permit their students to type their examinations. Before a student selects this alternative, he

---

* It should be mentioned that some professors might consider it improper to write *anything* prior to the instruction to commence the exam. While I never encountered this problem, perhaps it would be wise to confirm in advance that re-creation of a checklist after the test booklets are distributed, but before the actual direction to begin, is permissible. Of course, if a student is permitted to retain notes in his possession during the test, this problem would become moot.

might want to find out if there will be other typists in the same room. I chose to type the finals which were given at the close of the second semester, assuming that each typist would be assigned to an isolated area. However, all of the typists (approximately twelve) were placed in a single room. My analysis of the initial question had not been completed when the electric typewriter of another student went into operation, making it almost impossible to concentrate. I have read that many students who type their Bar answers wear earmuffs to diminish this problem. Another drawback of typing is that it is often very difficult to insert an issue or argument which was initially omitted, into the body of the answer. It is suggested that exams should be handwritten until a student acquires an understanding of what is involved.

Reading Instructions

Read the instructions carefully. The grader will not be impressed if you disregard his instructions to write on every other page or exceed the limitations pertaining to the length of the answer. Unbelievably, students frequently do not answer the question which is asked. If the bottom line of a hypothetical is, "What are X's rights against Y?", don't waste valuable time discussing Z's possible liability to X. If after the recitation of facts the question states something such as, "A sues B. Write the opinion of the court hearing this matter"; you should assume that the attorneys would have raised every legitimate issue. Therefore, the answer to this type of question would be written in the following form: "Although X contended that an enforceable contract was never formed because (1) . . . , (2) . . . , and (3) . . ." Occasionally, a question will pose the issue for the test-taker and inquire as to how it should be resolved. In such instances the grader will expect you to focus upon the arguments, pro and con, which each side would tender and discuss why those of one are more convincing than those of the other.

Before actually reading the hypotheticals, you should take a quick glance to determine if the professor has indicated the approximate amount of time which should be devoted to each question. There is sometimes a statement such as "Suggested Time: 50 Minutes" immediately above or below each question. Since there is usually a direct correlation between the suggested time allocations and the grading weight which will be given to a particular question, it would be wise to undertake the hypotheticals with the longest recommended times first. If a time overrun does then occur, the answers of lesser significance will suffer (it is better to achieve an A on the question worth 70% and B on the one worth 30%, rather than vice-versa). If you realize that you cannot possibly finish the examination within the allotted time; first, outline the remaining issues (leaving a few lines between each one), and then go back and insert, as far as possible, the arguments which would be raised pertaining to such issues.

Understanding the Question

Opinions differ as to how much time should be spent analyzing a question before actually putting pen to paper. Responses to this question usually run between 25% to 40%

of the allotted time. It is submitted that approximately one-third of the time allocated to a particular hypothetical question should be devoted to reading and outlining the answer. This will usually provide sufficient opportunity to read the question thoroughly, yet permit a complete written answer. Each sentence may contain several issues; therefore, every word must be scrutinized. As a general rule, it is probably wise to read a hypothetical at least three times before beginning. It is suggested that as you discover each issue, draw a line emanating from the word or phrase which triggers it to the margin, with an abbreviation of that issue at the line's end.

Examination questions sometimes instruct the test-taker to assume that the events described in the hypothetical took place in the state of "Utopia" or some other mythical jurisdiction. Such a statement is basically equivalent to a declaration that there is no law on point in the state where the facts occurred. Such a pronouncement is relevant because if there has been an opinion in the casebook (obviously from an appellate court in one of the fifty states) which strongly supports the position of one of the parties on a particular issue, it would not have to be followed by a court of Utopia since the principle of *stare decisis* is applicable only to courts within one jurisdiction. The decisions of courts in other states may be adopted, but there is no compulsion to do so. While the side which was favored by a particular opinion would certainly allude to it in his or her answer, the other would begin his or her remarks by reminding the grader that the courts of Utopia are free to promulgate a contrary, more enlightened rule of law. Thus, an instruction of the type alluded to above opens the way for argument upon a given issue even though there is clear precedent on that point.

You will probably discover that during your first reading of a hypothetical, certain issues will be strikingly obvious. In your anxiety to discuss the issues which you readily perceive, you may fail to analyze the question carefully, and as a result, overlook latent problems. A law student must approach each hypothetical in a systematic, methodical manner. Recognizing the applicability of every possible major area and the potential issues inherent therein is important for several reasons: (1) issues or defenses which negate one cause of action or doctrine may not be applicable to another (i.e. an action for Defamation may fail because the plaintiff cannot demonstrate pecuniary loss, but actual monetary damage is *not* essential to a recovery for Invasion of Privacy), (2) the greater the possible grounds of recovery, the greater the likelihood of obtaining some type of relief, as well as a greater recovery, and (3) a competent attorney is expected to assert every possible argument or defense which will further his or her client's cause.

When to Make Assumptions

The instructions on a final may instruct you to "assume" whatever facts are deemed necessary to answer the question in a complete manner. Even where such express authorization is not given, you may be obliged to make certain assumptions with respect to missing facts to write an intelligent answer. Assumptions, when used correctly can be an important ally since they often permit you to eliminate potential issues in an expeditious manner and thereby save valuable time. One of my fellow students at Columbia once reduced an ostensibly complex Civil Procedure question pertaining to jurisdiction and venue to the proverbial *cakewalk* by making a few skillful assumptions as to the residence, domicile and place of business of the various parties involved. However, the reader must be forewarned that assumptions must be employed carefully because unjustified assumption indicates a substantial lack of understanding of the course materials. Assumptions should *never* alter or modify the given facts.

Assumptions can legitimately be made only when they are necessary to write a thorough and complete answer. For example, to sustain a defamation lawsuit the plaintiff in most instances is required to prove that he or she suffered some type of monetary damage as a result of the defendant's remarks or actions. If the facts presented in the test hypothetical are completely silent as to this point, a student should expressly state something such as, "It is assumed that plaintiff can show that defendant's communications caused some type of economic damage to him (i.e. loss of job, a dinner invitation, etc.)." The foregoing would demonstrate to the grader that the test-taker is aware that pecuniary loss is an essential element to a successful cause of action for defamation, and also resolves this point in a terse manner.

Three Common Test Errors

There are probably three major errors committed by freshmen law students on final examinations. The first is failure to discuss every possible major area which is applicable to a particular question. *Where two or more causes of action are applicable to the circumstances described in a hypothetical, each must be discussed.* In a Torts hypothetical, for example, it is essential to discuss every possible cause of action upon which liability might be established. The facts which give rise to a false imprisonment lawsuit often also support assault and battery actions . Similarly, the circumstances set forth in a Criminal Law hypothetical often present several potential offenses for which the defendant can be charged. Your answer should encompass all of them. In Evidence there are numerous reasons why a statement may not be admissible (i.e. irrelevancy, hearsay, privilege, etc.), all of which should be examined. To reiterate, reviewing old exams should heighten your awareness of overlapping doctrines.

Another costly error is neglecting to follow an answer through. *When responding to a hypothetical it is essential to assume that each issue would be resolved by a Court in a manner which would necessitate consideration of the next issue.* Suppose a student recognizes that a Contracts' question involves issues pertaining to offer, termination, acceptance and consideration. Regardless of how strongly you believe that the alleged offer was merely an invitation or too indefinite and therefore the plaintiff could not possibly prevail, you should *not* terminate your answer after a discussion of just these issues. Similarly, even though the test-taker feels strongly that a certain piece of evidence will be inadmissible on one theory (i.e. hearsay), all other grounds which might serve as a basis for excluding it should also be discussed. In the same vein, students sometimes discuss the substantive issues, but omit questions pertaining to "who is liable for what, and for how much." Thus, answers to hypotheticals involving negligence often cover the basic allegations and defenses to such an action, but fail to go into topics such as vicarious liability, damages, and contribution rights between joint tortfeasors.

It should constantly be kept in mind that law school exams are designed with the objective of testing your ability to isolate and discuss the issues which are embedded in an alien factual situation. Therefore, very few genuine issues are not susceptible to legitimate differences of opinion as to how they should be resolved. As noted in the discussion following *Katko* v. *Briney*, even where there is a decision squarely on point, it would not have to be adopted by a court in any other jurisdiction. When you begin the actual practice of law, you will raise every possible issue and assert every possible defense, rather than put all of your eggs in one basket. A similar philosophy should be adhered to when taking law exams. As previously noted, well-organized checklists should automatically lead a student through *all* of the main doctrines and principles (and the issues inherent therein) of each major area.

The third type of recurring flaw is the failure to discuss perceived issues. You may discern a legal controversy, but ignore it because you believe it would obviously be resolved in favor of one side or the other, and is therefore not worthy of mention. For example, if in a Torts hypothetical involving negligence there are issues pertaining to standard, duty, foreseeable consequences, and damages, you should not omit discussion of the duty problem simply because you are fairly certain that the plaintiff would be able to carry his or her burden of proof on this element. If you are confident, but not absolutely positive, that no genuine issue exists, the matter should be disposed of in a line or two by stating something such as, "under the circumstances set forth in the hypothetical, the defendant clearly had a duty to the plaintiff." Before an issue is precluded in this manner, however, the question must be analyzed carefully to verify that there are no off-setting arguments which a sympathetic court could adopt to reach a contrary result. *It must never be assumed that the grader is tuned into your mental processes. All non-frivolous issues merit discussion.*

Test-Taking Techniques

If the first reading of a hypothetical leaves you completely lost, don't panic. This will rarely occur if you have reviewed exams from prior years. Go back to the major areas (at least one of which will be applicable), and reconsider each of their parameters. Then read the question again. If you still come up with a blank, probably the best thing to do is proceed to the next hypothetical. You will most likely realize which doctrines were applicable to the earlier question in a short while.

Don't waste time on non-issues. If Mr. X deliberately hit Mr. Y on the head with a bottle, there is little doubt that the technical elements of a battery are present. However, X might not be liable if his actions were done in self-defense (i.e., Y was menacing him with a knife). If this was the situation, you should not bother describing or defining a battery; instead, you should commence immediately with the first genuine issue. Thus, you would begin your exam with a statement such as: "The initial issue is whether X's Battery upon Y was privileged on the grounds of self-defense?".

It is also important to remember to treat both sides of each issue with equal intensity. If the hypothetical describes how a destitute widow is evicted from her home by a rich oil company, your sympathies might understandably fall on the side of the former. Despite the moralities of such a situation, the grader will expect you to make every possible argument and rebuttal which would be made on behalf of the oil company. The point is, you should never permit your personal viewpoint to subconsciously affect your answer. When discussing an issue, always play the devil's advocate.

Students sometimes forget to make sufficient reference to the factual situation present in the question. Legal principles are merely skeletons until animated by the circumstances set forth in a hypothetical. For example, whether a defendant "acted like a reasonable person" or "impugned" the plaintiff's character, will depend almost exclusively upon the relevant facts. Thus, the resolution of the issues in one way or the other will often be dependent solely upon the facts. As noted earlier, a slight twist in the circumstances of a hypothetical may bring into play entirely new principles and arguments. *While ingenious theoretical arguments will undoubtedly impress the grader, you should not lose sight of the importance of demonstrating the interaction between the pertinent facts and the applicable rules of law.*

It is usually a good idea to leave a blank line between each written line, even when not required by the instructions. This will usually make the answer easier to read, and facilitates the insertion of material which you may remember while reading over your answer. Although it is difficult to calculate, a messy test answer must have a negative psychological impact upon someone who is grading a great number of papers. Finally, abbreviations may be utilized to save time. A simple way to show that a term or word is being shortened is by placing your abbreviation between parentheses and quotation marks immediately after the word the first time you use it. Thus, the word "reasonable" could be reduced to "r" on an exam in the following manner—reasonable ("r"). Many possible abbreviations are indicated on the checklists found on the preceding pages.

Open-Book Finals

Open-book tests became prevalent during my last semester of law school. The most appropriate response to this phenomenon was aptly described by my first year legal advisor at Columbia. He stated to me that, "The best thing is *not* to bring your books or summaries to the exam. If you do, the very next best thing is to place them at the upper portion of your desk and *not* open them during the exam." Unfortunately, some students are undoubtedly lulled into a sense of euphoria when they are informed that their finals will be open-book, believing the gaps in their knowledge can be filled by a quick reference to their notes.

This approach is wrong. As emphasized throughout this work, to successfully attack hypothetical-type exams your emphasis in law school must be upon understanding and analysis rather than memorization. You will not be able to answer finals by simply *plugging-in* your notes as you may have done on the undergraduate level. Also, an inevitable loss of time and concentration will result when it becomes necessary to sift through the casebook and notes for specific information. Although you should bring the casebook to the exam since a particular question might refer the test-taker to a specific page, it is strongly suggested that you should not plan to alter study techniques as described in the foregoing pages because the final is open-book. Only the checklists, which would have been re-created anyway, should be referred to during an exam.

Epilogue

If for any reason you are unable to reach the academic goals set for yourself in the freshman year despite many hours of hard work, don't become discouraged. What happens many times, unfortunately, is that students who fail to make the Law Review* or are otherwise disappointed with their grades tend to resign themselves to an unnecessarily low level of academic performance. Such a relatively negative approach undoubtedly results in less than complete fulfillment of your legal potential. If you permit yourself to subconsciously adopt this attitude, you will be perpetrating a great disservice upon yourself.

It is highly questionable whether there is any correlation between your grade-point average in law school and your achievements as a practicing attorney. While native intelligence undoubtedly plays a role in recognizing and solving legal problems, by far the major factor which will determine your success as an attorney is diligence (i.e. researching all of the applicable law, discovering the material facts, and staying with a difficult problem or situation even though the odds are sometimes against a successful resolution). It should also be remembered that first-year courses may represent a small fraction of the type of legal work you may ultimately do. Courses pertaining to the law of corporations, evidence, secured real and personal property transactions, collection, etc., are usually offered only *after* the initial year. In fact, since there is an interval of at least two years between your freshman courses and actual legal

* This is usually the law school equivalent of Dean's List.

practice, much of what you learned in the first year must usually be relearned anyway.

There are several things that you can do to enhance your chances of obtaining the desired position after graduation, despite less than sensational marks in your freshman year. First, you can achieve high grades throughout the remainder of your law school career. Many institutions have recently adopted procedures whereby it is possible to become a member of some type of scholarly entity *after* the freshman year. Another means of promoting your legal stature is to write articles on topics of interest. If you are too preoccupied with your regular studies during the academic year, you can use the intervening summers for this purpose. Regardless of whether your work is published in a law review or in a practitioner-oriented magazine (i.e. state or local bar journal), undertaking such a project demonstrates a willingness to do something beyond the norm as well as an expertise in a particular subject. If you are unable to think of a topic, consult your professor. Writing articles should also sharpen your research skills which, as noted earlier, are often very important to potential employees.

I was chagrined when my extensive first-year efforts produced an unsatisfactory academic yield. Despite these initial disappointments, I continued to put in the long hours of concentrated work which are required for a good legal education. I must believe that if I had allowed myself to form a *B student* self-image, my grades would have continued at that level, and in turn, I would not presently be practicing the type of law and with the kind of people I enjoy. Unless you do everything in your power to make the most of your legal education, you will never know if your true potential has been realized.

As advised in the initial chapter, this book should be read in its entirety before law school commences, and then reviewed as you become more familiar with the legal materials which are discussed. Examples from Torts and Contracts' law were utilized since these are invariably freshman year subjects, which the reader should be able to relate to early in the initial semester. The crucial thing to remember is that there are a finite number of potential issues for each course, and they can arise in just so many ways. The quicker you acquire the *feel* for organizing and understanding the context in which the prospective issues are likely to appear on an exam, the more likely is academic success in law school.

It is sincerely hoped that the foregoing pages have not made law school seem like a totally grim proposition. Although the hours of study were long and the pressures sometimes intense, in retrospect, I view my legal education as sort of a fun time. Unlike actual practice, there are few deadlines to meet (finals are usually given once or twice each academic year), there are usually no dress requirements (I have been compelled to forego my faded jeans and workshirt during business hours), and there is a great degree of flexibility in choosing associates (it is highly doubtful that you will turn away prospective clients because of some personality foible). Most enjoyable, however, was the opportunity to become immersed in the purely theoretical aspect of the law. Despite the rigors of law school, you will probably look back at that period someday with a surprising amount of fondness. Good luck!

Appendix

To give the reader some examples of actual law school exams and to demonstrate the basic similarity of hypothetical tests, the Appendix contains finals given at Columbia University School of Law (in New York) and the University of Southern California School of Law.

The following series of exams were given at Columbia.

TORTS—L6118x
Final Examination — January, 1975
Professor Hill
Time Allowed — Four Hours

PLEASE ENTER NAME OF COURSE AND INSTRUCTOR'S NAME ON EXAM BOOK. ANSWERS MUST BE WRITTEN IN INK OR TYPEWRITTEN.

Instructions:

This is a *limited open-book* examination. You may bring into the examination room your casebook, case-briefs prepared by you, and your notes, but you are cautioned against spending a significant amount of time with these materials.

Assume that you are in a jurisdiction which does not have decisions bearing squarely on the issues raised by the questions. Everything you have read is therefore relevant insofar as pertinent; but no case or other authority need be cited by name. A "no fault" statute has not been

adopted in the jurisdiction. In discussing the rights of
the parties you should of course consider significant defenses that might be raised. What is wanted is the kind
of rounded and reasoned answer, complete with recom-
mendations, which would be helpful to an employer.

Observe the space limitations. A "page" is one side of a
sheet in the answer book; allowance is made for hand-
writing that is particularly large or small. For those who
are typing, a "page" is about 150 words. You will have
no trouble in conforming to the space limitations if you
spend at least half of your time planning your answers
and outlining them on scrap paper. You have been given
abundant time precisely in order that you may have a
significant opportunity to think about your answers.

If you believe that additional facts are needed, or that a
question is defective for any reason, make any assumptions you deem appropriate, stating what they are.

The grading of the examination will proceed one question
at a time. Since your answers will not be read consecu-
tively, you should not assume that, in the grading of a
particular answer, account will be taken of statements
made in other parts of your answer book. Each answer
should be self-contained.

There is no comparative negligence statute.

I

[Space Limitation: Four Pages]

Mary Doe and Sally Peter were rivals for the presidency
of the PTA of the local junior high school. Mrs. Doe de-
spised and hated Mrs. Peter, as numerous witnesses are
prepared to testify. Among other things, Mrs. Doe has said

of Mrs. Peter that as a high school senior (some twelve years earlier), she, Sally Peter, had posed in the nude for a "shady" magazine. This remark was made by Mrs. Doe at a bridge game, at which the other players were a member of the same PTA, a woman from the same school district whose children were beyond school age, and a woman from a neighboring school district. It has since been learned that Mrs. Doe obtained the information from a private detective specially retained by her to investigate Sally Peter; the detective had made inquiries in the distant state where Sally Peter grew up, but in this instance he may have confused Sally Peter with her indisputably wild sister, Polly.

Your law firm has been retained by Sally Peter, and the foregoing information has been given to you with instruction to prepare a memorandum on her rights—first, on the assumption that the charge of having posed in the nude for a "shady" magazine is false; and, second, on the assumption that the charge is true. Do not consider the possible liability of the detective. (In this school district, a PTA is an unofficial organization comprised of the parents of school children and such teachers as choose to join.)

II
[Space Limitation: Four Pages]

Acme Construction Co. had contracted to add two additional lanes to a heavily-used highway in a rural area. To establish the proper grade, Acme had occasion to engage in blasting, since there was much solid rock on or close to the surface.

Signs at the side of the road, at the approaches to the blasting area, warned motorists as follows: "Blasting in progress. Stop all radio transmissions." Baker, a motorist using his two-way radio, failed to observe the sign; there was a premature detonation which was caused, it may be assumed, by the transmission from his radio; and in the ensuing explosion Baker was injured when a boulder hit his car.

Charles, a motorist who stopped at the scene of the accident and then hurried off to summon medical assistance (Baker's radio had been rendered inoperative), was killed when his car swerved from the road and hit a tree. Charles was not wearing his seat belt at the time. The car was so mangled that it was impossible to tell whether Charles would have been killed even if he *had* been wearing his seat belt, or whether the failure to wear the seat belt was a substantial contributing factor towards his death in that, if suitably restrained by the seat belt, Charles would have escaped fatal secondary impact after his car hit the tree. A statute makes it unlawful to manufacture or sell an automobile unless equipped with seat belts for occupants of the front seat. (Charles's car was not one of those, produced in recent years, that "refuse" to start if the seat belts are not engaged.)

Discuss (1) the rights of Baker; and (2) the rights of those with standing to sue for Charles's death under the pertinent wrongful death statute.

III
[Space Limitation: Four Pages]

Paul is not very bright, but fortunately he is well off financially. About a year ago he decided to resume the violin lessons that he had taken briefly as a child. At about the same time, he met Jones, a noted concert violinist, at a reception, and asked Jones to recommend a dependable concern which sold fine violins. Jones replied that Paul could deal "in absolute confidence" with one John Sterling.

So Paul went to Sterling's establishment. He waited while another buyer conducted negotiations with Sterling for a violin, which was spoken of as a "Gaspard Schlumberger," and which was apparently deemed to have special value on that account. The negotiation was unsuccessful, and the first buyer left. Paul then asked to see the same violin, examined it as well as he could, and asked Sterling whether the violin was indeed a "Gaspard Schlumberger." Sterling replied: "That is my understanding." Paul bought the violin for $5,000. The bill of sale did not identify the violin as a "Gaspard Schlumberger," and contained a clause to the effect that the buyer did not rely on any representations other than representations expressly set out in the bill of sale. It may be assumed that the presence of this clause precludes successful suit for breach of contract, or for breach of warranty (assuming the latter to be something distinct from breach of contract).

Subsequently, it developed that the violin was not a "Gaspard Schlumberger," but of inferior make; and that Sterling had disappeared and could not be found despite intense effort. It also developed that Jones, prior to vouching for Sterling, had heard a rumor attributing sharp practice to Sterling, but had discounted the rumor on the basis of his own extensive dealings with, and impression of, the man.

Paul told his story to Snipe, a lawyer, who advised Paul not to be concerned about the disappearance of Sterling, since there was "a very strong case" against Jones. Paul gave Snipe a $500 retainer fee, and left the violin with Snipe. Subsequent inquiries by Paul brought uninformative replies and demands for more money. The total payments to Snipe aggregate $1500; and Paul had just about decided to refuse further demands for money when news came that a fire in Snipe's building, occurring without fault on Snipe's part, had resulted in destruction of the violin.

Paul has now taken his troubles to the law firm that employs you, and you have been asked to prepare a memorandum on his rights. You have been told all of the foregoing, and, in addition, that Sterling has been located.

CONTRACTS
Final Examination — May, 1975
Professor Rosenthal
Time allowed — 3½ hours
ANSWERS MUST BE WRITTEN IN INK OR TYPED.

This is an *open-book* examination. You may use any materials brought for your exclusive use. If nothing more, *you must bring to the examination the casebook assigned in the course.*

The provisions of the Uniform Commercial Code (as they appear in the Supplement) are assumed to be enacted law in any jurisdiction concerned.

There are four questions. At the head of each there is a suggestion of the time believed to be ample for your answer. This is for your guidance only. The total is less than the time allowed.

Your answers should take the form of ordinary exposition. Sensible paragraphing will be sufficient to indicate the several parts of an answer. Please do not introduce an answer with a list of the issues to be canvassed.

There is no space limitation as such; but if you can do so conveniently, please confine your answers to a single blue book. You may use both sides of a page, and if your script is not more than ordinarily illegible single spacing is acceptable.

I
A Case of Shingles
(1 hour, 15 min.)

The Ronson Roofing Company obtained a subcontract to

do all the roofing work on a projected "retirement village," an extensive housing development for senior citizens. The design for the village calls for slate shingles to be employed wherever, in the architect's judgment, slate would enhance the desired Old World effect. Otherwise Ronson is permitted to use a cheaper material: any fireproof shingle that will satisfy the building code.

One of the few sources for slate shingles is the Slippery Shingle Company. Suitable slate is not available near the site except at Slippery's works, in the State of Hysteria. Shipping costs from other sources are considerable. The only practicable way of extracting slate is by open-pit (strip) mining.

In February Ronson placed a contract with Slippery for the purchase of 50,000 square yards of shingles, for delivery at the construction site as needed over the summer. The contract specified prices for both slate and composition shingles, and called for Ronson to designate the type desired in each shipment order.

In March the legislature of Hysteria took up a bill to prohibit strip mining in the state from June 1 forward. Political insiders gave the bill a good chance of enactment. Ronson was immediately aware of the threat to its position from this bill. It wrote as follows to Slippery:

March 15 (Ronson to Slippery): We are concerned about the possible effect on you of House Bill 007. Is it true that, if passed, the bill would force you to cease the production of slate shingles? In view of this possibility, we think we are entitled to definite assurance that you will honor your commitment to us in connection with the Over-the-Hill Village project. Please advise promptly.

Slippery answered as follows:

You are correct that our supply of slate is in jeopardy,

owing to the proposed legislation. However, we have a considerable quantity of slate shingles either warehoused or in production, and if worst comes to worst we mean to fill every order that we possibly can.

We note that you have not given us the quantity of your requirement of slate. If you want us to reserve for you the full contract quantity of slate shingles, or some definite part of it, you should declare the quantity to us by the end of the month. If you miss this deadline, we cannot assure you of full satisfaction. Our policy will be to fill orders received after this month on the basis, first come, first served.

Ronson received this letter on March 20. It wrote back at once, saying that Slippery's answer was unsatisfactory:

March 20 (Ronson to Slippery): We are not able to state our requirements of slate until the architect completes his detailed design specifications. We estimate that at least 30,000 yards of slate will be needed. Unless you confirm your commitment in full, *immediately*, we shall take protective action, as our lawyer advises.

On April 1 Ronson wrote to the Cover Shingle Company, of Fartown, for a quotation on slate shingles, and sent a copy to Slippery. The price quoted, f.o.b. Fartown, was $10 a yard—$2 more than the price in the Slippery contract. Shipping costs to the Village would add a dollar a yard more to Ronson's cost.

On April 15 Slippery sent Ronson a firm offer (UCC 2-205), good for one month, to supply 20,000 yards of slate shingles at $10 a yard, delivered at Over-the-Hill Village.

House Bill 007 was sent to the Governor of Hysteria late in April and he signed it on May 1.

On May 10 the architect for the Village provided Ronson with specifications for roofing that required 40,000 yards of slate shingles. On May 15 Ronson contracted with Cover for that quantity, delivered at the Village, at $12 a yard. No better price was then available, except under Slippery's offer.

At the same time, Ronson mailed Slippery an acceptance of its April 15 offer.

Slippery has refused to deliver any slate shingles to Ronson, and has disclaimed any liability for breach of contract. What are Ronson's rights against Slippery? Explain.

II
The Case of the Aggressive Agent
(35 min.)

Please consult *Beattie-Firth, Inc.* v. *Colebank*, at p. 634 of the casebook. For this question you are to assume the facts of that case as pleaded by the plaintiff, together with additional facts as follows. Ben Beattie, the president of Beattie-Firth, acted for his company in dealing with the Colebanks and with Carl Anderson. In its name he executed the agreements of July 7 and August 20, 1956.

After the circuit court sustained the Colebanks' demurrer, instead of appealing the plaintiff, Beattie-Firth, filed an amended declaration. According to the declaration as amended, all the parties concerned met on August 20, at the plaintiff's office, to execute the sale contract. Shortly before the signing, Anderson stepped out of the room to telephone his lawyer. In his absence, Ben Beattie said to the Colebanks,

> You know, I have an idea that guy [Anderson] might try to welsh on his agreement. What do you think?

Harry Colebank answered: "Well, I don't know, but if he does you will have his $500 for your trouble." Beattie said: "If he does I think you should hold his feet to the fire. Would you be willing to go after him for the rest of the money? I tell you what: if you promise to do that I'll agree that my firm will pay half the lawyer's fee, and you can pick the lawyer." Harry said, "It's a deal. Ruth and I don't want to have to show the house to any more Sunday lookers."

At that, Anderson returned to the room and the agreement, as described in the opinion, was signed by the three parties.

In 1957 (still according to the plaintiff's amended declaration), when Anderson announced he would not complete the purchase, Ben Beattie urged the Colebanks to engage a lawyer and sue for specific performance. They refused, however, to do so. The present action, Beattie-Firth v. Colebank, followed.

The defendants demurred again to the declaration as amended. How should the circuit court rule on the demurrer? Explain.

III
The Case of the Mare Margie
(25 min.)

William Toney contracted to buy a quarter-horse named Miss Margene from Gary Lambarth. "Margie," as she was called, was a pretty little filly, a fine show lady. Her color was grulla and her disposition easy. Toney's object was to provide a show and racing horse for his daughter.

Toney paid $600 down and contracted in writing to pay $400 more within sixty days. The contract provided, however, that

This purchase is contingent upon examination by a veterinarian of Toney's choice and that such Dr. declare the mare above to be sound.

After an examination, the veterinarian selected reported as follows:

It is my professional opinion that the above described

mare is unsound because of blindness in her right eye.

/s/ Gerald Schrater, D.V.M.

While awaiting full payment, Lambarth kept possession of Margie as a boarder.

After the vet's report, Lambarth refused to return Toney's $600, and Toney sued him for it. The trial court, sitting without a jury, heard testimony that Margie was not blind, and was a champion pleasure horse. Dr. Schrater was asked about a soundness examination. His answer was:

A soundness examination consists of a physical examination to determine the health and physical condition of the horse for purchase; see if she is healthy, and the word in the horse world we use is "sound." Is she functional for the purpose intended?

The trial court found that Margie was sound in this sense, and gave judgment for Lambarth. Toney appealed.

What should the decision be? Explain.

[See Toney v. Lambarth, 514 S.W.2d 106 (Mo.App. 1974).]

IV

The ARC Case

(1 hour)

On two occasions the ARC Corporation (Magnetic Products Division) ordered two shipments of circuitry from the Beta Engineering Corporation, each shipment to be paid for 90 days after receipt. The purchase orders, which Beta acknowledged, contained this provision:

Seller agrees to make no assignment of rights under this order without the prior written consent of ARC. In the event of such an assignment, Seller agrees to furnish ARC with two conformed copies of the instrument of assignment.

After filling the first order Beta gave an assignment of its right to the unpaid price, in the form of a "security agreement," as collateral for an advance made to Beta by the Eco Finance Corporation. No consent was sought from ARC. Eco promptly sent a notice of the assignment, identifying the purchase order by number, to ARC, by certified mail. The notice stated that Beta had also assigned—as it had—all other accounts receivable to Eco, "whether now owing or hereafter arising," as security for the loan. The notice directed ARC to make any payments earned by Beta directly to Eco. A dock attendant at ARC's divisional headquarters signed for the certified mail item, as he was authorized to do; but the notice never reached the accounting office.

Beta received the second purchase order from ARC a month later. Beta made a formal assignment to Eco under this order also, but Eco sent no further notification to ARC.

In due time ARC paid for its purchases by checks issued and mailed to Beta.

Eco now finds that Beta is insolvent, and unable to repay the loan. Fortunately for it, it holds guaranties of payment given by two officers of Beta: A. Gallivanter (treasurer) and C. Homebody (secretary). Gallivanter has decamped with Beta's money, and cannot be found. There remains Homebody, and he is your client.

It is possible, by the law of suretyship, that Eco's management of the collateral was so careless as to afford your client a partial or complete defense against Eco's claim. But that is far from certain. Eco has offered to settle with your client on these terms: Homebody pays Eco 80% of the unpaid balance on the loan, and Eco assigns to him any and all claims it may have against ARC. Homebody asks for your counsel about this proposal.

One further development may bear on your decision: ARC has discovered that the circuits in the second set shipped by Beta were seriously defective. As a result, it claims, it has had to make expensive adjustments with customers who received ARC products embodying these circuits.

[See Ertel v. Radio Corporation of America, 307 N.E.2d 471 (Ind. 1974). Note that, in this case, no wrongdoing is imputed to the departing official; the court says only that "his whereabouts are unknown, leaving Ertel to face the liability."]

PROPERTY—SECTION 2
L6116y
Final Examination — May, 1975
Professors C. Berger and V. Berger
Time Allowed — 3 Hours and 45 Minutes

IF YOU ARE A CANDIDATE FOR GRADUATION IN MAY, 1975, WRITE AT THE TOP OF YOUR FIRST PAGE "CANDIDATE FOR GRADUATION IN MAY, 1975."

This is a *limited-open-book* examination. You may consult only the Casebook, the printed and multilithed supplements, your notes, and any synthesis or outline that you have had a substantial part in producing.

Answers must be written in ink or typewritten. Use a separate answer book for each of the three questions. Write on only *one* side of the page.

I
(75 minutes)

On July 1, 1971, Vera Vane signed a lease on apartment 3D in High-Rise Manor, and entered into possession. The reserved rent was $400 a month; the lease was to run through June 30, 1974. Ms. Vane, a widow, had had qualms about paying so much rent. But because the landlord maintained a private playground on the premises where her four-year-old son Tommy could play with the other tenants' children, she finally decided to take the apartment.

All went well for the first year. Then, in the summer of 1972, Hilda Hassle moved in with her eight-year-old boy, Butch. Butch Hassle was a vicious bully, who would roam the playground unsupervised and pick fights with younger children. Several mothers complained to the landlord about Butch's uncontrolled behavior. After Butch knocked down and beat a toddler, several tenants circulated a petition which Ms. Vane, among others, signed. It read as follows:

"We, the undersigned tenants, demand that you evict Hilda Hassle because of the numerous assaults [an itemized list was appended] committed by her son on other tenants' helpless children. We know that you have the power to do so since her lease, like all of ours, says: 'Tenant and tenant's family shall at all times conduct themselves peaceably and in a manner respectful of the rights of other tenants.' "

Notwithstanding these efforts, however, the landlord took no action.

On September 15, 1973, Ms. Vane took Tommy to the playground. She became engaged in an animated discussion with some other mothers, and paid no attention to the child until she suddenly heard his screams. According to witnesses, Butch Hassle had crept up behind Tommy and—without warning—attacked him with a shovel. Tommy spent a week in the hospital, and Ms. Vane paid $900 for his medical bills.

The Vanes never again returned to the playground, and Ms. Vane began looking for another apartment. On October 1, she sent a check for $100 to the landlord, with the following explanation: "You owe me $900 on account of my son's injuries. I will deduct $300 a month from the rent until

this amount is made up. Signed—Vera Vane." The landlord refused to cash her check, whereupon Ms. Vane stopped
paying any rent at all. In the middle of December, Ms. Vane
finally found a comparable apartment for $350. On Decem-
ber 31, 1973, she and her son moved out for good.

You are a member of the Bar of the State of Kent. Harry
Homesly, the landlord, has retained you in this matter. Advise him of any claims he may have against Ms. Vane, and
possible means of enforcement. Evaluate Mr. Homesly's
chances for success, in light of the defenses *and/or counter-
claims* that Ms. Vane is likely to assert. (If you make any
factual assumptions, state what they are. With respect to
the law, draw on your general knowledge.)

II
(Suggested Time — 90 mins.)

H and W own a lot in Kent City as tenants by the entirety. The lot, which the couple acquired in 1965 for
$30,000, includes a large 8-room house and a 2-car garage.
W contributed the $30,000 from her winnings in a state
lottery. In 1967, the couple legally separated and H moved
to another city. The separation agreement privileged W
to use the house. In 1968, at a cost of $10,000, W illegally
converted the house into a 2-family dwelling and rented
one of the units to X who has lived there since July 1, 1968.
To finance the conversion, W borrowed $10,000 from her
father which she has since repaid with $1,000 interest.
X's 10-year lease expires June 30, 1978. X pays for heat
and utilities, makes all repairs, and pays W a monthly
rental of $300.

In addition to the dwelling unit, X has also occupied one
side of the 2-car garage—for storing furniture, as a work-
shop, and since 1970, for parking his car. The garage was
not included in the lease, however. Although W knew about
X's use of the garage and asked him several times to re-

move his things, X ignored her requests and W did not press the matter.

In 1975, H returns to Kent City for the first time since 1967 and learns about the conversion, the lease with X, and X's occupancy of the garage. H writes a nasty letter to W, demanding partition, a full accounting for H's share of rental and mesne profits, and damages for any losses he might suffer because of the illegal conversion and X's occupancy.

W seeks your advice. She reports having paid the entire real estate taxes and fire insurance premiums on the property since 1967. These have come to $1,000 and $200 yearly respectively.

The applicable statute for the recovery of real property has a 6-year limitations period, but is otherwise modeled after the New York law. The applicable statute for the recovery of contract damages has a 3-year limitations period.

Prepare a memorandum of law dealing with each of the issues raised by H's letter.

III
(Suggested Time — 60 mins.)

The Town of Keepaway sells 10 acres of residentially zoned surplus land to Y. The deed provides that Y shall build a high-rise condominium containing not more than 70 units. The deed also provides: "Y covenants, for himself and his assigns, to reimburse the Town for the tuition cost of all 'excess' children attending Town public schools. The tuition charge for 'excess' children shall be imposed in any year that more than 100 children from the project attend such schools. Unpaid charges shall be a lien against the property."

Y builds the 70-unit project. He keeps 5 units (which he

leases out) as an investment and sells all of the remaining units.

One year later, 125 children from the project are attending Town public schools. Pursuant to the deed provision, the Town assesses each occupant of the project $600. as the unit's proportionate share of the $42000 tuition cost for the 25 "excess" children. Letters notifying occupants of the assessment state:

"Pursuant to our July 1, 1970 agreement with Y, which is a covenant running with the land, you are hereby directed to remit $600. with 30 days to pay your unit's share of the 1974-75 tuition cost for 25 children attending Town public schools from the project. Failure to pay this charge promptly may result in a personal judgment against you and a lien against your unit."

The occupants consult you for an opinion as to their rights, duties, and liabilities. Prepare a memorandum carefully analyzing the issues that are presented by this set of facts. If you assume any additional facts, do so explicitly. Do not, however, assume away the entire question.

Examination Number

....

LEGAL METHOD—SECTIONS 1 and 2
L6113x
Final Examination — January, 1975
Professor Murphy

PLEASE ENTER NAME OF COURSE AND INSTRUCTOR'S NAME ON YOUR EXAM BOOK.

ANSWERS MUST BE WRITTEN IN INK—LEGIBLY— OR TYPEWRITTEN.

USE ONLY ONE SIDE OF EACH PAGE IN THE AN-
SWER BOOK.

TYPEWRITTEN PAPERS MUST BE DOUBLE-SPACED
WITH LEFT-HAND MARGINS OF AT LEAST 1½
INCHES.

INSTRUCTIONS: This is a *limited open-book* examination.
  You may refer to:
  a) The multilithed casebook used in the course—*Legal
     Method Cases and Materials*, Jones, Kernochan and
     Murphy (1974);
  b) Your own class notes and any other outlines or re-
     view materials prepared by you, alone or jointly
     with classmates. (Of course no *joint use* of notes
     is permitted.)

                *   *   *   *   *   *   *

You are reminded that this is an examination in legal
method and is designed to determine the extent to which
you can use the lawyer's methods and skills for the ac
complishment of practical, professional tasks. You will
be graded not only on your knowledge of the materials
and your ability to analyze fact situations but also on the
clarity and precision of your reasoning and the extent
to which your answers measure up to professional standards of clear organization and forceful expression. By all
means, *read* and *think* through each question before you
start to write your answer to it.

                            I
                [Suggested Time: 50 Minutes]
On April 13, 1973, Mr. J. Smith, a Connecticut resident,
was driving his new Mercedes automobile in a westerly direction on Swamp Road in Wachovia, New York. A truck

owned and operated by Ms. R. Able was pulling a trailer along Swamp Road in the opposite direction. The truck was attached to the trailer by a "pintle hook," or "coupler" which had been sold to Able by its manufacturer, Hooks Co. ("Hooks"), a New York company. As the truck and Smith's car were approaching each other, Smith was adjusting his rear view mirror. Just before they passed each other the pintle hook parted, and the trailer—becoming detached from the truck—crossed onto the left side of the road and collided with the oncoming car. The car was almost totally demolished as was an extremely valuable vase Smith had just purchased; but, miraculously, Smith was not injured.

Smith brought suit in the United States District Court for the Northern District of New York against Able, claiming she had negligently attached the trailer to the coupler, and against Hooks, claiming that the accident was caused by a defect in the coupler. At the close of the case, the judge granted Able's motion for a directed verdict but denied a similar motion by Hooks.

At the request of Smith's counsel, the judge charged the jury that, if they found that the pintle hook had been defectively made and that the trailer had become uncoupled from the truck because of that defect, they must find for the plaintiff. The judge refused the request of Hooks' counsel to charge the jury that unless they found that the defect in the coupler was the result of Hooks' negligence they should bring in a verdict for Hooks; he also refused a request to charge that if the jury found that plaintiff had not operated his car with reasonable care they must find for Hooks.

Hooks' counsel duly excepted to the charge and to the denial of his requests for charges. The jury brought in a verdict for Smith in the amount of $23,000 for his automobile and his vase.

Hooks has appealed to the Court of Appeals for the Second Circuit, claiming that the charge and the denials of his counsel's requests to charge were erroneous. You are an Associate in the firm of Crooke and Crooke. The senior Mr. Crooke, as counsel for Hooks, asks you to write a memorandum on the law governing this case.

Your customary assiduous researches unearth, in addition to the cases in the Legal Method materials, the following per curiam opinion rendered in 1965 by the New York Supreme Court, Appellate Term, Second Department:

"BERZON ET AL., Respondents v. DON ALLEN MOTORS, INC., Appellant, Appeal from a judgment of the New York City Court, King's County—Order unanimously reversed, with costs and motion granted to the extent of dismissing the fifth and sixth causes of action in the complaint. Memorandum: Plaintiffs were pedestrians who were struck by a truck manufactured by defendant General Motors Corporation and sold to defendant City of Buffalo by defendant-appellant Don Allen Motors, Inc. The accident is alleged to have resulted from failure of the truck's brakes. The complaint alleges six causes of action. We are concerned on this appeal only with the fifth and sixth causes of action in which recovery is sought from appellant for breach of implied warranty relating to the truck's braking mechanism. The Court below denied appellant's motion to dismiss these two causes of action citing *Goldberg* v. *Kollsman Instrument Corp.* (12 N.Y.2d 432) as authority for sustaining their sufficiency. The principle enunciated in *Goldberg* created liability on the part of the vendor (appellant) "for breach of law-implied warranties, to the persons whose use is contemplated." In *Thomas* v. *Leary* (235 N.Y.S. 2d 137 [App. Div. 4th Dept. 1964]), it was held that an employee of the purchaser would be such a contemplated user and should be protected under the implied warranty doctrine as "a logical and progressive step" in the application of the *Goldberg* doctrine. We decline to extend Goldberg to this case. To do so would be such a radical departure from established law that if it is to be accomplished it should be done by legislative action and not judicial pronouncement."

Prepare the memorandum asked for by Mr. Crooke. Be sure to deal with any arguments which you think will be made by opposing counsel.

II

[Suggested Time — One Hour and Twenty Minutes]

A transportation bond issue was submitted for approval to the voters of the State of Kent at the 1973 general election. The bond issue was a bipartisan matter in that support or opposition was not determined along regular political party lines. The Kent Legislature had enacted it by a substantial majority (drawn from "both sides of the aisle") subject to its approval by the voters. It was recognized, however, that such bond issues are often rejected by the voters and the proponents of this bond issue organized a not-for-profit corporation called YES FOR TRANSPORTATION IN KENT, INC. (known as "YES" for short) to promote its approval. YES collected some $2.5 million in individual and corporate donations and expended all these funds in its campaign. Despite the best efforts of YES and other supporters—including the Governor of Kent who urged the bond issue as a source of jobs and activator of growth—the bond issue was defeated at the polls.

One of the organizations contributing to YES was the Kent Telephone Company (KT), a subsidiary of AT&T. In fact, KT provided $50,000 to YES in support of the bond issue. As justification for this contribution, KT's directors argued that KT had a substantial interest in the transportation bond issue, stemming from its vast pool of 12,000 motor vehicles using the State's highways and from its huge work force dependent in large numbers on effective arrangements for mass transportation.

KT's contribution to YES in relation to the public referendum was objected to by the Organization on the Social Responsibility of Corporations (OSROC) which was a shareholder of KT. OSROC demanded that the directors of KT recover the contribution (or if that was not possible repay the amount of the contribution to the corporation) on the ground that such a contribution contravened § 40 of the Kent Election Law. Countering the pro-contribution arguments of the directors, OSROC suggested that their motivation might have been to curry favor with the Governor of Kent as the officer charged with appointing members of the Public Service Commission from which KT hoped to procure rate increases. The directors of KT, relying on the advice of counsel that the contribution was not illegal, refused OSROC's demand. OSROC then brought a civil action against KT's directors to require recovery or repayment of the contribution. In the trial court, summary judgment was given for OSROC, based on a finding that KT's contribution had violated § 40. The case was appealed and is now before the Kent Court of Appeals (the highest appellate court of Kent).

Assume you are clerk to one of the judges of the Kent Court of Appeals who has asked you to prepare a memorandum—in effect a draft opinion—covering the case of OSROC v. Directors of KT. You are to assume also that the sole question before the Court is whether or not KT's contribution violated § 40. It is stipulated that all procedural requirements for presenting this question for decision have been properly met.

The text of § 40 of the Kent Election Law reads in pertinent part as follows:

"§ 40. *Political contributions prohibited; penalty; witnesses' privilege.*

"No corporation or joint-stock association doing business in this state, except a corporation or association organized or maintained for political purposes only, shall directly or indirectly pay or use any money or property for or in aid of any political party, committee or organization, or for, or in aid of, any corporation, joint-stock or other association organized or maintained for political purposes, or for, or in aid of, any candidate for political office or for nomination for such office, or for any political purpose whatever, or for the reimbursement or indemnification of any person for moneys or property so used. Any officer, director, stockholder, attorney or agent of any corporation or joint-stock association which violates any of the provisions of this section, who participates in, aids, abets or advises or consents to any such violation, and any person who solicits or knowingly receives any money or property in violation of this section, shall be guilty of a misdemeanor."

Your careful and thorough research disclose only the following additional material that may be pertinent to the present case:

1. Webster's Third New International Dictionary defines "political" in part in these terms:

"1a: of or relating to government, a government, or the conduct of governmental affairs; b: of or relating to matters of government as distinguished from matters of law. . . ; c: engaged in civil as distinguished from military functions . . . ; d: of, relating to or concerned with the making as distinguished from the administration of governmental policy . . . ; 3a: of, relating to, or concerned with politics; b: of, relating to, or involved in party politics. . . ."

2. The origin of § 40 is traceable to a proposal made in 1894 for an amendment to the Constitution of the State of Kent. The proposed amendment, which was not adopted, read thus:

> No corporation shall directly or indirectly use any of its money or property for, or in aid of, any candidate for political office, or for nomination for such office, or in any manner use any of its money or property for any political purpose whatever, or for reimbursement or indemnification of any person for moneys or property so used.

Its sponsor, when challenged as to its breadth, explained his proposal as follows in the State Constitutional Convention:

> The idea of this section, Mr. Chairman, is to prevent the great moneyed corporations—the great railroad companies, insurance companies, telephone companies, etc.—from furnishing money to political candidates or parties, directly or indirectly, to elect legislators or executive officers to vote or act for the protection of corporate interests as against those of the public. . . .
> The time has come to put a stop to the giving of $50,000 or $100,000 by a great corporation for political purposes, on the understanding that a debt is thereby created from a political figure or party, a debt to be repaid in votes or administrative action. . . ."

3. § 40 was enacted in its present form in 1906 as a result of a report by the Kent Legislature's Joint Interim Committee on Insurance Problems, detailing instances of corporate contributions to political parties and candidates for political purposes. In its Report, the committee stated:

Contributions by insurance corporations for political purposes should be strictly forbidden . . . whether made for the purpose of supporting or imposing political views or with the desire to obtain protection for the corporation, these contributions have been wholly un-justifiable. They should be expressly prohibited and treated as a waste of corporate moneys, without the consent of the stockholders whose political views may differ from those of the directors. Moreover, any officer or director participating in any such contribution should be guilty of a misdemeanor.

4. The former Chairman of the above-mentioned Joint Interim Committee, in a 1912 letter to the Kent State Superintendent of Insurance, stated in relation to § 40: "We sought, and provided for, a broad coverage of corporate activities in the political process so as to leave no room for the evils aimed at."

5. When § 40 was enacted there was also before the Legislature at that time a competing proposal which was allowed to die in committee and which would, *inter alia*, have explicitly barred contributions for "any question to be voted on at an election."

6. § 120 (also adopted in 1906) of the Kent Election Law provides for the public reporting of the contributions of "any committee or combination of three or more persons cooperating to aid or to promote the success or defeat of a political party or principle or of any proposition submitted to vote at a public election."

7. § 66 of the Kent Legislative Law, also adopted in 1906, recognizes the right of a corporation to retain lobbyists to promote or oppose the passage of bills or resolutions or to promote or oppose executive approval thereof—subject to a requirement of public disclosure of the amounts paid to such lobbyists.

8. The Attorney General of the State of Kent, as an intervenor on this appeal, has advised the Kent Court of Appeals that his office—as the agency charged with responsibility for applying the Election Law—has on occasion, orally and informally advised interested parties that § 40 does not apply to referenda.

9. § 95 of the Kent Business Corporation Law authorizes a corporation "to make donations, irrespective of corporate benefit, for the public welfare and for civic or similar purposes."

PREPARE A COMPACT WELL-ORGANIZED MEMORANDUM (DRAFT OPINION) FOR THE JUDGE FOR WHOM YOU ARE A CLERK

(A) INDICATING THE STATUTORY ISSUE OR ISSUES RAISED,

(B) GIVING YOUR RECOMMENDED DECISION ON SUCH ISSUE OR ISSUES, AND

(C) JUSTIFYING YOUR DECISION AND DEALING WITH EACH ITEM OF THE RESEARCH MATERIALS LISTED ABOVE AND WITH THE PROBABLE ARGUMENTS OF COUNSEL FOR OSROC AND COUNSEL FOR THE KT DIRECTORS.

III

[Suggested Time — Fifty Minutes]

Gambling establishments may operate lawfully under state licenses in the State of Columbia. Section 100 of the Columbia Statutes provides in pertinent part:

"It is hereby declared to be the policy of this state that all establishments where gambling games are conducted or operated . . . shall be licensed or controlled so as to better protect the public health, safety, morals, good order and general welfare of the inhabitants of the State of Columbia."

Such licensing has existed since at least 1870, when the

above-noted provision was enacted. Licensed gambling is taxed by the State and produces such substantial revenues (over half the State's income) by way of taxes and license fees that Columbia has found it unnecessary to impose income taxes upon its citizens.

Ms. Lotta Doe, a citizen of Columbia, spent a few hours some months ago at a card table in the Acme Casino, which is a licensed gambling establishment located in Columbia and operated by a Columbia corporation (Acme Casino, Inc.). Her losses to the Casino on this occasion amounted to $13,800. Upset by these losses, Ms. Doe was led to investigate. From her own and other inquiries thereafter she gathered highly persuasive evidence showing that the Casino had used marked cards against her to insure that the Casino would win.

Ms. Doe brought an action against Acme Casino, Inc. in the appropriate trial court of the State of Columbia. Her complaint alleged the above facts, including Acme's use of marked cards, and demanded recovery of the $13,800. Defendant Acme filed a motion to dismiss on the ground that the complaint failed to state facts sufficient to constitute a cause of action. Defendant's motion to dismiss was granted by the trial court. As permitted by the applicable law of Columbia, plaintiff Doe appealed to the Supreme Court of Columbia, the State's highest court.

Assume you are a judge of the Supreme Court of Columbia assigned to write an opinion in the case of *Doe* v. *Acme Casino, Inc.*, ruling on the correctness of the lower court's action in granting Acme's motion to dismiss. You are to assume that all procedural prerequisites for the Supreme Court's ruling on the question whether this motion should have been granted have been properly met.

In addition to the facts and law already set forth above, research supplies you with the following:

(1) In *Carr* v. *Parke*, 7 Columbia 419 (1872), plaintiff, owner of a licensed gambling house, sued to recover a gambling debt owed by defendant. Affirming a judgment for defendant, the Court held the principles of the common law barring such a recovery remained applicable in Columbia. It said, *inter alia*: "The statute [licensing gambling house] does not pretend to do more than to protect the keepers of public gaming houses from criminal prosecution when a proper license is procured."

(2) In 1920, in the case of *Green* v. *Jones*, in the Rhino County Court of the State of Columbia, plaintiff sought to recover losses from a defendant who had allegedly used loaded dice against plaintiff in an informal, private and unlicensed dice game at defendant's private home. The Court dismissed the complaint for failure to state a claim upon which relief could be granted. The Court in this case, which was not appealed, said in pertinent part: "We follow the settled principles of the common law. Those who gamble do so at their own risk. They may not invoke the help of the courts when they are burned toying with fire."

(3) Section 183 of the Columbia Statutes, enacted in 1913, makes it a misdemeanor punishable by fine or imprisonment, or both, to use in any licensed gambling game "bogus or counterfeit chips, cards or dice that have been marked, loaded or tampered with," or other devices designed to fetter the whims of Lady Luck.

(4) In *Smith* v. *Freedom Casino*, 71 Columbia 283 (1956), plaintiff gambler sued defendant, a licensed gambling casino, alleging failure and refusal to pay him sums he had won at roulette.

Affirming a dismissal of the complaint for failure to state a claim upon which relief could be granted, the Columbia Supreme Court said: "We hold, as we did in *Carr* v. *Parke, supra,* and as the County Court did in *Green* v. *Jones, supra,* that people who gamble may not seek the aid of the courts when they are displeased with the results of these activities. Though they are licensed, gambling houses are not favored enterprises in the eyes of the law. Those who frequent them are not normally entitled to the law's solicitude."

(5) In *Todd* v. *Rose,* decided in 1970 by the Rhino County Court of Columbia, plaintiff, a private citizen, was refused the aid of the Court in his effort to collect from defendant, another private citizen, sums allegedly won by plaintiff in a wagering transaction.

DRAFT A COMPACT, WELL-ORGANIZED OPINION
(A) GIVING YOUR DECISION AS TO WHETHER THE MOTION TO DISMISS SHOULD BE GRANTED OR DENIED;
(B) INDICATING THE ISSUE OR ISSUES RAISED;
(C) JUSTIFYING YOUR DECISION ON THE ISSUE OR ISSUES RAISED AND DEALING WITH THE ARGUMENTS THAT WOULD PROBABLY HAVE BEEN MADE ON SUCH ISSUE OR ISSUES BY COUNSEL FOR DOE AND COUNSEL FOR ACME.

INSTRUCTIONS TO STUDENTS
CRIMINAL LAW—SECTION 1
L6108y
Final Examination — May, 1975
Professor Wechsler

ANSWERS MUST BE WRITTEN IN INK OR TYPE-
WRITTEN.

IF YOU ARE A CANDIDATE FOR GRADUATION IN
MAY, 1975, WRITE ON THE COVER OF YOUR AN-
SWER BOOK OR AT THE TOP OF YOUR FIRST PAGE
"CANDIDATE FOR GRADUATION IN MAY, 1975."

This is a take-home examination. It is not a research
project. Although you may consult anything inanimate
that you wish, the questions may all be fully answered
solely on the basis of the course materials and discussions.

You may not under any circumstances discuss the questions with others until the examination period has ended
on *Wednesday, May 14.* Nor may you in any other way
give or receive aid in answering the questions.

I plan to grade these examinations on an anonymous
basis. Accordingly, you will have received an examination number when you picked up this examination, and
you should display this number at the top of your answer
to *each* question. Please begin your answer to each question on a separate page. Your name should not appear
anywhere on your answer.

It is recommended that you keep a copy of your examination answer in the unlikely and unhappy event an
examination answer should be lost.

The examination should be handed in to the Chief Proctor
in Room F no later than 2:00 p.m. on Wednesday, May
14. If you complete the examination before this time, you

may hand in your answers to the Chief Proctor in Room F any time during regular examination hours.

In writing your answers do not exceed the specified maximum length.

There is a premium on clarity, brevity, organization and good English prose.

CRIMINAL LAW—SECTION 1
L6108y
Final Examination — May, 1975
Professor Wechsler
I
[Space maximum: 1500 words]

The proposed Federal Criminal Code now pending in Congress (S. 1, 94th Cong., 1st Sess.) deals with federally cognizable homicide as follows:

"§ 1601. Murder

"(a) OFFENSE.—A person is guilty of an offense if:

"(1) he engages in conduct that knowingly causes the death of another person;

"(2) he engages in conduct that causes the death of another person under circumstances in fact manifesting extreme indifference to human life; or

"(3) in fact during the commission of an offense described in section 1101 (Treason), 1102 (Armed Rebellion or Insurrection), 1111 (Sabotage), 1121 (Espionage), 1313 (Escape), 1601 (a) (1) or (a) (2) (Murder), 1611 (Maiming), 1621 (Kidnapping), 1622 (Aggravated Restraint), 1625 (Aircraft Hijacking), 1631 (Rape), 1701 (Arson), 1711 (Burglary), or 1721 (Robbery) that he commits either alone or with one or more other participants, he or another person engages in conduct that in fact causes the death of a person other than one of the participants in such underlying offense.

"(b) AFFIRMATIVE DEFENSES.—It is an affirmative defense to a prosecution under:

"(1) subsection (a) (1) that the death was caused under circumstances, for which the defendant was not responsible, that:

"(A) cause the defendant to lose his self-control; and

"(B) would be likely to cause an ordinary person to lose his self-control to at least the same extent;

"(2) subsection (a) (3) that the death was neither a necessary nor a reasonably foreseeable consequence of:

"(A) the underlying offense; or

"(B) the particular circumstances under which the underlying offense was committed.

"(c) GRADING.—An offense described in this section is a Class A felony.

"§ 1602. Manslaughter

"(a) OFFENSE.—A person is guilty of an offense if:

"(1) he engages in conduct that causes the death of another person; or

"(2) he engages in conduct that knowingly causes the death of another person under circumstances that would constitute an offense under section 1601 (a) (1) except for the existence of circumstances in fact constituting an affirmative defense under section 1601 (b) (1).

"(b) GRADING.—An offense described in this section is a Class C felony.

"§ 1603. Negligent Homicide

"(a) OFFENSE.—A person is guilty of an offense if he engages in conduct that negligently causes the death of another person.

"(b) GRADING.—An offense described in this section is a Class D felony."

The general provisions of the proposed Code relevant to the meaning and application of the homicide provisions are as follows:

"§ 301. State of Mind Generally

"(a) STATE OF MIND DEFINED.—As used in this title, 'state of mind' means the state of mind required to be proved with respect to conduct, an existing circumstance, or a result set forth in a section describing an offense.

"(b) TERMS USED TO DESCRIBE STATES OF MIND.— The terms used to describe the different states of mind are 'intentional', 'knowing', 'reckless', and 'negligent', and variants thereof.

"(c) STATES OF MIND APPLICABLE TO CONDUCT, AN EXISTING CIRCUMSTANCE, AND A RESULT.—The states of mind that may be specified as applicable to:

"(1) conduct are either 'intentional' or 'knowing';

"(2) an existing circumstance are either 'knowing', 'reckless', or 'negligent'; and

"(3) a result are either 'intentional', 'knowing', 'reckless', or 'negligent'.

"§ 302. 'Intentional', 'Knowing', 'Reckless', and 'Negligent' States of Mind

"The following definitions apply with respect to an offense set forth in any federal statute:

"(a) 'INTENTIONAL'.—A person's state of mind is intentional with respect to:

"(1) his conduct if it is his conscious objective or desire to engage in the conduct;

"(2) a result of his conduct if it is his conscious objective or desire to cause the result.

"(b) 'KNOWING'.—A person's state of mind is knowing with respect to:

"(1) his conduct if he is aware of the nature of his conduct;

"(2) an existing circumstance if he is aware or believes that the circumstance exists;

"(3) a result of his conduct if he is aware or believes that his conduct is substantially certain to cause the result.

"(c) 'RECKLESS'.—A person's state of mind is reckless with respect to:

"(1) an existing circumstance if he is aware of a risk that the circumstance exists but disregards the risk;

"(2) a result of his conduct if he is aware of a risk that the result will occur but disregards the risk.

The risk must be of such a nature and degree that its disregard constitutes a gross deviation from the standard of care that a reasonable person would exercise in such a situation.

"(d) 'NEGLIGENT'.—A person's state of mind is negligent with respect to:

"(1) an existing circumstance if he ought to be aware of a risk that the circumstance exists;

"(2) a result of his conduct if he ought to be aware of a risk that the result will occur.

The risk must be of such a nature and degree that the

failure to perceive it constitutes a gross deviation from the standard of care that a reasonable person would exercise in such a situation.

"§ 303. Proof of State of Mind

"Except as otherwise expressly provided, the following provisions apply to an offense under any federal statute:

"(a) REQUIRED PROOF OF STATE OF MIND.—A state of mind must be proved with respect to each element of an offense, except that:

"(1) no state of mind must be proved with respect to any element of an offense if the description of the offense does not specify any state of mind and the offense is:

"(A) an infraction; or

"(B) an offense described in a statute outside this title, or in a regulation or rule issued pursuant to such a statute; and

"(2) no state of mind must be proved with respect to a particular element of an offense if that element is specified in the description of the offense as existing or occurring 'in fact'.

"(b) REQUIRED STATE OF MIND FOR AN ELEMENT OF AN OFFENSE IF NOT SPECIFIED.—Except as provided in subsection (a), if an element of an offense is described without specifying the required state of mind, the particular state of mind that must be proved with respect to:

"(1) conduct is 'knowing';

"(2) an existing circumstance is 'reckless'; and

"(3) a result is 'reckless'.

"(c) SATISFACTION OF STATE OF MIND REQUIREMENT BY PROOF OF OTHER STATE OF MIND.—If the state of mind required with respect to an element of an offense is:

"(1) 'knowing', this requirement can be satisfied alternatively by proof of an 'intentional' state of mind;

"(2) 'reckless', this requirement can be satisfied alternatively by proof of an 'intentional' or 'knowing' state of mind;

"(3) 'negligent', this requirement can be satisfied alternatively by proof of an 'intentional', 'knowing', or 'reckless' state of mind.

"(d) MATTERS OF LAW REQUIRING NO PROOF OF STATE OF MIND.—

"(1) EXISTENCE OF OFFENSE.—Proof of knowledge or other state of mind is not required with respect to:

"(A) the fact that particular conduct constitutes an offense or is required by or violates a statute or a regulation, rule, or order issued pursuant thereto;

"(B) the fact that particular conduct is described in a section of this title; or

"(C) the existence, meaning, or application of the law determining the elements of an offense.

"(2) JURISDICTION, VENUE, AND GRADING MATTERS.—Proof of state of mind is not required with respect to any matter that is solely a basis for federal jurisdiction, for venue, or for grading.

"(3) MATTERS DESIGNATED A QUESTION OF LAW.—Proof of state of mind is not required with respect to any matter that is designated as a question of law.

"§ 401. Liability of an Accomplice

"(a) LIABILITY IN GENERAL.—A person is criminally liable for an offense based upon the conduct of another person if:

"(1) he knowingly aids or abets the commission of the offense by the other person; or

"(2) acting with the state of mind required for the commission of the offense, he causes the other person to engage in conduct that would constitute an offense if engaged in personally by the defendant or any other person.

"(b) LIABILITY AS COCONSPIRATOR.—A person is criminally liable for an offense based upon the conduct of another person if:

"(1) he and the other person are coconspirators;

"(2) the other person engaged in the conduct in furtherance of the conspiracy; and

"(3) the conduct was a reasonably foreseeable consequence of the conspiracy.

"§ 501. Application and Scope of Bars and Defenses

"The bars and defenses to prosecution set forth in this chapter are not exclusive, but the general subject matters covered in this chapter constitute bars or defenses to prosecution only to the extent described in this chapter.

"§ 521. Mistake of Fact or Law

"It is a defense to a prosecution under any federal statute that, as a result of ignorance or mistake concerning a matter of fact or law, the defendant lacked the state of mind required as an element of the offense charged. Except as otherwise expressly provided, ignorance or mistake concerning a matter of fact or law does not otherwise constitute a defense.

"§ 522. Insanity

"It is a defense to a prosecution under any federal statute that the defendant, as a result of mental disease or defect, lacked the state of mind required as an element of the offense charged. Mental disease or defect does not otherwise constitute a defense.

"§ 523. Intoxication

"(a) DEFENSE.—It is a defense to a prosecution under any federal statute that the defendant, as a result of intoxication, lacked the state of mind required to be proved as an element of the offense charged if:

"(1) intent or knowledge is the state of mind required; or

"(2) recklessness or negligence is the state of mind required and his intoxication was not self-induced.

Intoxication does not otherwise constitute a defense.

"(b) DEFINITIONS.—As used in this section:

"(1) 'intoxication' means a disturbance of a mental or physical capacity resulting from the introduction of alcohol or a drug or other substance into the body;

"(2) 'self-induced' intoxication means intoxication caused by a substance that the actor knowingly introduces into his body with knowledge that it has, or with reckless disregard of the risk that it may have, a tendency to cause intoxication.

"§ 531. Duress

"It is an affirmative defense to a prosecution under any federal statute, other than a prosecution under section 1601 (Murder), that the defendant engaged in the conduct charged because another person coerced him to do so by a clear threat of imminent and inescapable death or serious bodily injury to himself or to any other person, if:

"(a) the threat was of such a nature as would render a person of reasonable firmness in the position of the defendant incapable of resisting the coercion; and

"(b) the defendant had not:

"(1) intentionally, knowingly, or recklessly, if intent or knowledge or recklessness is the state of mind required to be proved as an element of the offense charged; or

"(2) negligently, if negligence is the state of mind required to be proved as an element of the offense charged; entered into a criminal enterprise or otherwise placed himself in a situation in which it was foreseeable that he would be subjected to coercion.

§ 541. Exercise of Public Authority

"(a) DEFENSE.—It is a defense to a prosecution under any federal statute that the conduct charged was required or authorized by law:

"(1) to carry out the defendant's authority as a public servant, or as a person acting at the direction of a public servant; or

"(2) to make an arrest as a private person.

"(b) DEADLY FORCE.—The use of deadly force is not justified under this section unless:

"(1) the defendant was a public servant authorized to make arrests, or a person acting at the direction of such a public servant, and the use of deadly force was reasonably required under the circumstances to arrest or prevent an escape from arrest of a person who:

"(A) had engaged in, or had attempted to engage in, conduct constituting an offense that involved a risk of death, serious bodily injury, rape, or kidnapping; or

"(B) was attempting to escape by the use of a weapon;

"(2) the defendant was a public servant with custody over a person being held in official detention; such person was not known by the defendant to be held in official detention other than as a result of a charge or conviction of an offense involving a risk of death, serious bodily injury, rape, or kidnapping; and the use of deadly force was reasonably required under the circumstances to prevent an escape of such person; or

"(3) the defendant was a public servant, and the use of deadly force was otherwise authorized by law.

"§ 542. Protection of Persons

"(a) DEFENSE.—It is a defense to a prosecution under this title for an offense involving the use of force against a person that the use of such force was reasonably required under the circumstances to protect the defendant or another person from:

"(1) the unprovoked use of unlawful force by such person; or

"(2) the use of unlawful force provoked by a fight or an affray that was entered into mutually if:

"(A) the defendant withdrew from the fight or affray and indicated to the other person that he had withdrawn, or

"(B) the other person unexpectedly resorted to the use of deadly force.

"(b) DEADLY FORCE.—The use of deadly force is not

justified under this section unless the use of such force was reasonably required under the circumstances to protect the defendant or another person from a risk of death or serious bodily injury. The fact that the defendant could have avoided using deadly force by retreating, with complete safety to himself and others, is a circumstance to be considered with all other circumstances in determining whether such force was reasonably required.

"§ 543. Protection of Property

"(a) DEFENSE.—It is a defense to a prosecution under this title for an offense involving the use of force against a person that the defendant had custody or possession of real or personal property and that the use of such force was reasonably required under the circumstances to prevent or terminate a trespass upon such property,or an unlawful taking of or damage to such property, by such person.

"(b) DEADLY FORCE.—The use of deadly force is not justified under this section.

"§ 544. General Provisions for Subchapter E

"(a) DEFINITIONS.—As used in this subchapter:

"(1) 'deadly force' means force that, under the circumstances, is likely to cause death or serious bodily injury;

"(2) 'force' means any physical interference with another person, including restraint;

"(3) 'unlawful force' means force used against another person in a manner constituting an offense under this title."

"(b) EFFECT OF MISTAKE.—A defense under section 541, 542, or 543 is available to a defendant if he believed that the factual situation was such that the conduct charged was required or authorized as set forth in the section describing the defense, even though he was mistaken in his belief, unless his belief was the result of recklessness or negligence and such recklessness or negligence is the state of mind required to be proved with respect to the pertinent element of the offense charged."

As law assistant to a United States Senator, your opinion is requested as to whether (a) in determining the criminality of homicide and in grading the homicidal crimes the proposed Code presents a serious danger of injustice; and (b) if so, what amendments he should offer to improve the bill.

What would you advise?

II

[Space maximum: 500 words]

Assume that the conduct involved in the following cases took place after the enactment of the provisions of the proposed Federal Criminal Code set forth in Question I in a jurisdiction subject to the Code. Should the conduct be held to constitute a crime and, if so, what offense? If your answer turns upon a jury's resolution of an issue of fact, state what the issue is.

1. Fain v. Commonwealth, Casebook p. 29.
2. Viliborghi v. State, Casebook p. 70.
3. People v. Caruso, Casebook p. 162.
4. People v. Schmidt, Casebook p. 814.

III

[Space maximum: 400 words]

You are an Assistant District Attorney working in the complaint bureau in New York County. In the course of a day's work the following two cases are presented, in which you are satisfied that the facts stated can be proved beyond a reasonable doubt.

1. D had a checking account in the Exchange Bank in which he usually maintained a balance of $1500. His monthly statement for March 31, 1975, showed a balance of $2100, including a deposit of $600 on March 17, which D did not in fact make. On April 9, D drew a check for $2000, leaving a balance of $100 in the account. On April 15, the Bank discovered the erroneous credit and notified D, requesting payment. D paid at once by a check drawn on another bank.

2. D, an attorney, told P, his client, that he needed certain stock certificates belonging to P to enable him to make out P's income tax return. A few days after P delivered the certificates, D stated that if P would endorse them to D, P might be able to avoid paying a tax on the dividends. P executed the endorsement while the certificates were lying on D's desk, upon D's promise to return them on demand. The next day, December 1, 1974, D applied for a bank loan and offered to pledge the stock as collateral for the loan. The bank agreed to make the loan but told D that in view of his high standing at the bar no collateral would be required. D immediately returned the securities to P, stating that he had concluded that no purpose would be served by the endorsement. D's bank loan is now overdue and is unpaid.

Is there in either of the cases a basis for criminal prosecution? If so, for what offense or offenses?

IV

[Space maximum: 300 words]

D and J rented an old farmhouse in an isolated area in New Jersey and set themselves up as distillers. They did most of the work themselves but arranged for X and Y, two farm boys in the neighborhood, to come in on Mondays,

Wednesdays and Fridays to help operate the stills. They also employed Z, an elderly maiden lady, as a housekeeper and cook. D and J failed to pay the Government tax on any of the spirits distilled; and it is clear that their intention was to operate without making such payment. X and Y, had no idea whether or not a tax was due on the liquor manufactured but D told them not to tell anyone there was a still on the farm and they followed his instruction. Z suspected that D and J were engaged in some shady business but, as she had no other place to live, she decided to mind her business and keep her job.

A federal statute declares it to be a felony "to distill any alcoholic beverage with intent to defraud the United States of the tax due thereon." D, J, X, Y and Z are jointly indicted in the United States District Court for violating this statute and also for conspiracy so to do. At the close of the evidence, the trial court is satisfied that a jury must reasonably find the facts stated above and can not reasonably find otherwise. Should he permit the case to go to the jury as to X, Y and Z and, if so, under what directions?

V

[Space maximum: 300 words]

In United States v. Braun, 382 F. Supp. 214 (S.D.N.Y. 1974), Judge Frankel rendered the following opinion on a motion for reconsideration of sentence:

On September 4, 1974, the defendant in this case, a young, perhaps excessively ambitious businessman, was sentenced to a relatively short term of imprisonment for attempted tax evasion. Four days later, on Sunday, September 8, 1974, the 38th President of the United States granted "a full, free, and absolute pardon unto" the 37th President of the United States "for all offenses against the United States which he, Richard Nixon, has committed or may have committed or taken part in during the period from January 20, 1969, through August 9, 1974." The court has been driven to consider whether these events may be thought to have any meaningful relationship to each other.

The defendant before us, who has moved for a reduction of sentence, is a man of 35. He has no prior criminal record. He is talented, gainfully employed, earnest in the discharge of family obligations, and entitled to hope for a bright, if unsung future. He needs no "rehabilitation" our prisons can offer. The likelihood that he will transgress again is as close to nil as we are ever able to predict. Vengeance, the greatest texts tell us, is not for mortal judges. Why, then, should such a man be sentenced to imprisonment at all?

That question, always the hardest at the time of sentencing, was not made easier by the fact that the crime in question (to which this defendant made a full public confession of guilt without a trial) occurred over six years ago. The court is told—and knows in any event— that the defendant has suffered terribly in the intervening years of investigation, uncertainty, legitimate efforts to avoid indictment, the awful decision to plead guilty, and the tortured wait for the day of sentence. This particular defendant, we learned on impressive professional opinion, has experienced some unique agonies under the emotional stress of criminal prosecution. "The defendant has suffered enough already" is a familiar refrain to sentencing judges. But the familiar is not necessarily contemptible. The refrain tells a true and moving story. Prison sentences are imposed in spite of it, for presumably weightier reasons, not because the griefs of a convicted defendant before sentence are unreal or trivial.

Why, indeed, then, a prison term for the defendant

before us? The grounds, for better or worse, may be recalled briefly: First, *general deterrence,* to make good the law's threats in the hope or belief that others will be discouraged from evading their taxes by the force of this example among many others. Second, *denunciation,* the recording of society's outraged disapproval in a case so serious that, in the words of a classic statement, a lesser penalty would "depreciate the seriousness of the defendant's crime."[1] Third, the demands of *equal justice;* increasingly, the courts recognize that "respectable" or so-called "white-collar" crimes must not be treated with benign understanding while our less privileged (and more driven) criminals serve long terms of imprisonment.[2]

But how do we reconcile the application of these factors to our unknown defendant with the pardon granted last Sunday? In the case at bar, the defendant's crime may have involved as much as $22,000 or as little as $2,500 in evaded taxes. The alleged crimes embraced by the recent pardon may have included among the lesser items tax evasion to the extent of several hundreds of thousands of dollars. This was, of course, a matter of relative insignificance in the course of conduct for which impeachment had been recommended. Comparison of the cases in terms of what might "depreciate the seriousness" of the crimes would, obviously, be ludicrous. And whatever is meant when we say

---

[1] Model Penal Code § 7.01 (1) (c).

[2] A lawyer like concern for accuracy compels an aside to say that some current generalities about "white collar" versus "blue-collar" crime are swift and uncritical. The armed robber and the embezzling bank official are likely to be dissimilar in an array of respects relevant to sentencing. But all of that is not vital for today's concerns in the case at hand.

comparisons are "odious," comparisons are the daily essence of our efforts to be fair and just.

As for "deterrence," the cases of the former President and of our defendant are different, to be sure, but scarcely in any way that makes it comfortable to be harsher here. We are entitled to hope that motivations loftier than the threat of prison will prompt our Presidents to execute the laws faithfully, to promote rather than obstruct justice, and to pay their taxes. But it remains a source of queasiness to realize that deterrence means "making examples" of people (despite the moral and philosophic questions that raises) ; that our relatively anonymous defendant adds at most to a mass of indistinguishable examples; and that the alleged example of a topmost leader has been declared immune by the pardoning power.

There remains, among others, the question whether and when a defendant has "suffered enough." Attempts to measure relative suffering must commonly be, and would be in the present case, grossly inexact and unsatisfactory. The agonies of a President, exposed to the glare of daily publicity and the thunder of daily attack, are surely unparalleled by the travails of inconspicuous people caught in the criminal process. On the other hand, fairness would demand a huge discount for the corollary facts that a President has sought the spotlight, won it along with the trust and hopes of the people, and therefore became exposed to what he and everyone would expect when charges of betrayal were brought. A President falls from, because he has been raised to, a dizzying height. Except to know that the qualities of many experiences are magnified and deepened by his position, we have no scale on which to weigh his sorrows against those of others.

The question about "equal justice" continues to demand an answer. (The quoted phrase is essentially redundant, however familiar. The word "justice" must entail "equality," though that does not exhaust its meaning.) The ideal is not easily reached. It is not achieved by treating everyone alike. The objectives are to treat "like" people alike while taking account of meaningful differences. Where differences are discerned —between people or their crimes or both—they are to be justly appraised. The armed robber is different from the shoplifter, the impoverished thief from the rich embezzler, the professional from the passionate offender, the petty miscreant from the violator of high trust. The differences suggest value judgments as to where the weight of severity should fall.

Making the comparison thrust upon us by recent events, it is difficult to tip the balance against the defendant before us. And yet the answer must in the long run be clear: if people in high (or even the highest) places may on occasion have been dealt with too easily, the remedy is not to loosen the bonds of law and decency for all of us. It is to resolve that we shall strive more earnestly, at every level, to enforce the rule of equality under the law.

Having thought recently on this subject in a comparable case, this court wrote:

"We are, for much more than a slogan, a government 'of the people'. We are not led by any permanent or sacred aristocracy, anointed to do its will and pronounce our standards, good or evil, from on high. To be sure, we look for leadership to those we select. But we select them. And in the end it is we who govern them, not they who govern us. The Supreme Court recalled a while ago, and we do well never to forget, two bedrock propositions as James Madison declared them for us:

'The people, not the government, possess the absolute sovereignty.'

* * * * * * *

'If we advert to the nature of Republican Government, we shall find that the censorial power is in the people over the Government, and not in the Government over the people.'[1]

"It follows that the missteps of people in power are no excuse, and should be no cause, for our breaking faith with ourselves. Wrongdoers in high places and low must be brought to justice. Whether or not that ideal is always achieved, our standards of law and morality are rooted in the people. If the poet may be paraphrased without disrespect, it is to ourselves, not the occasionally fallen star, that we must look for the preservation and steady renewal of our deepest values."[2]

We adhere to those views for the long run. But the defendant before the court neither lives nor pleads in a long run. He is here short days after Sunday, September 8, 1974. Sentencing, as reflected in the title of a recent and valuable book,[3] is still an exceedingly "human process"—variable, disorderly, riddled with the uncertainties produced by the differences among well-meaning judges. The judges of this Circuit, assembled in annual conference, spent much of last weekend brooding together over the grim subject of "disparities" in sentencing. Many were driving home from those ses-

---

[1] New York Times Co. v. Sullivan, 376 U.S. 254, 274, 275, 84 S.Ct. 710, 723, 11 L.Ed. 2d 6S6 (1964).

[2] United States v. Paterno, 375 F.Supp. 647, 648 (D.C., 1974).

[3] J. Hogarth, Sentencing as a Human Process (1971).

sions when the pardon of last Sunday was announced.
We may pretend, but can never manage entirely, to
ignore such juxtapositions of events in the imposition
of sentence. Certainly the people sentenced cannot be
expected to ignore them. And we must pay attention
to their sense of justice too—not least of all on the
ground taught by Saint Thomas Aquinas, that the person punished must, if possible, be moved to "accept"
his affliction as the just consequence of a just system.

Having tried to review the many pertinent factors,
and having recorded some major portions of the effort, the court concludes that in the particular case at
bar, at this particular time, the prison sentence cannot
justly be executed. Accordingly, the motion for reconsideration will be granted, execution of the prison
sentence will be suspended, and defendant will be
placed on probation for a period of one year in addition to paying the fine of $1,000 heretofore imposed.

(1) Was it appropriate for the court to accord the weight
that it did to the Nixon pardon?

(2) Apart from the Nixon pardon, is a sentence of imprisonment defensible in such a case?

The following examinations were given at the University
of Southern California Law School.

USCLS-12/74: Final Examination—LAW, LANGUAGE &
ETHICS (512) Dec. 16, 1974

. . . .

Petitioners McGautha and Crampton were convicted of
murder in the first degree in the courts of California and
Ohio respectively and sentenced to death pursuant to the
statutes of those States. In each case the decision whether
the defendant should live or die was left to the absolute

discretion of the jury. We granted certiorari limited to the question whether petitioners' constitutional rights were infranged by permitting the jury to impose the death penalty without any governing standards. For the reasons that follow, we find no constitutional infirmity.

A. McGautha's Guilt Trial

McGautha and his codefendant Wilkinson were charged with committing two armed robberies and a murder on February 14, 1967. In accordance with California procedure in capital cases, the trial was in two stages, a guilt stage and a punishment stage. At the guilt trial the evidence tended to show that the defendants, armed with pistols, entered the market of Mrs. Pon Lock early in the afternoon of the murder. While Wilkinson kept a customer under guard, McGautha trained his gun on Mrs. Lock and took almost $300. Roughly three hours later, McGautha and Wilkinson held up another store, this one owned by Mrs. Benjamin Smetana and operated by her with her husband's assistance. While one defendant forcibly restrained a customer, the other struck Mrs. Smetana on the head. A shot was fired, fatally wounding Mr. Smetana. Wilkinson's former girl friend testified that shortly after the robbery McGautha told her he had shot a man and showed her an empty cartridge in the cylinder of his gun. Other evidence at the guilt stage was inconclusive on the issue as to who fired the fatal shot. The jury found both defendants guilty of two counts of armed robbery and one count of first-degree murder as charged.

B. McGautha's Penalty Trial

At the penalty trial, which took place on the following day but before the same jury, the State waived its opening, presented evidence of McGautha's prior felony convictions and sentences and then rested. McGautha testified in his own behalf at the penalty hearing. He admitted that the murder weapon was his, but testified that he and Wilkinson had traded guns, and that it was Wilkinson who had struck Mrs. Smetana and killed her husband. McGautha testified that he came from a broken home and that he had been wounded during World War II. He related his employment record, medical condition, and remorse. He admitted his criminal record but testified that he had been a mere accomplice in two of those robberies and that his prior conviction for murder had resulted from a slaying in self-defense. McGautha also admitted to a 1964 guilty plea to a charge of carrying a concealed weapon. He called no witnesses in his behalf.

The jury was instructed in the following language:

"in this part of the trial the law does not forbid you from being influenced by pity for the defendants and you may be governed by mere sentiment and sympathy for the defendants in arriving at a proper penalty in this case; however, the law does forbid you from being governed by mere conjecture, prejudice, public opinion or public feeling.

"The defendants in this case have been found guilty of the offense of murder in the first degree, and it is now your duty to determine which of the penalties provided by law should be imposed on each defendant for that offense. Now, in arriving at this determination you should consider all of the evidence received here in court presented by the People and defendants throughout the trial before this jury. You may also consider all of the evidence of the circumstances surrounding the crime, of each defendant's background and history, and of the facts in aggravation or mitigation of the penalty which have been received here in court.

". . . Notwithstanding facts, if any, proved in mitigation or aggravation, in determining which punishment shall be inflicted, you are entirely free to act according to your own judgment, conscience, and absolute discretion. That verdict must express the individual opinion of each juror.

"Now, beyond prescribing the two alternative penalties, the law itself provides no standard for the guidance of the jury in the selection of the penalty, but, rather, commits the whole matter of determining which of the two penalties shall be fixed to the judgment, conscience, and absolute discretion of the jury."

We consider first McGautha's and Crampton's common claim: that the absence of standards to guide the jury's discretion on the punishment issue is constitutionally intolerable. To fit their arguments within a constitutional frame of reference petitioners contend that to leave the jury completely at large to impose or withhold the death penalty as it sees fit is fundamentally lawless and therefore violates the basic command of the Fourteenth Amendment that no State shall deprive a person of his life without due process of law. Despite the undeniable surface appeal of the proposition, we conclude that the courts below correctly rejected it.

In recent years academic and professional sources have suggested that jury sentencing discretion should be controlled by standards of some sort. The American Law Institute first published such a recommendation in 1959. Several States have enacted new criminal codes in the intervening 12 years, some adopting features of the Model Penal Code. Other States have modified their laws with respect to murder and the death penalty in other ways.

None of these States have followed the Model Penal Code and adopted statutory criteria for imposition of the death penalty. In recent years, challenges to standardless jury sentencing have been presented to many state and federal appellate courts. No court has held the challenge good.

It is apparent, moreover, that even such criteria as have been proposed do not purport to provide more than the most minimal control over the sentencing authority's exercise of discretion. They do not purport to give an exhaustive list of the relevant considerations or the way in which they may be affected by the presence or absence of other circumstances. They do not even undertake to exclude constitutionally impermissible considerations. And, of course, they provide no protection against the jury determined to decide on whimsy or caprice. In short, they do no more than suggest some subjects for the jury to consider during its deliberations, and they bear witness to the intractable nature of the problem of "standards" which the history of capital punishment has from the beginning reflected. Thus, they indeed caution against this Court's undertaking to establish such standards itself, or to pronounce at large that standards in this realm are constitutionally required.

In light of history, experience, and the present limitations of human knowledge, we find it quite impossible to say that committing to the untrammeled discretion of the jury the power to pronounce life or death in capital cases is offensive. The States are entitled to assume that jurors confronted with the truly awesome responsibility of decreeing death for a fellow human will act with due regard for the consequences of their decision and will consider a variety of factors, many of which will have been suggested by the evidence or by the arguments of defense counsel. For a court to attempt to catalog the appropriate factors in this elusive area could inhibit rather than expand the scope of consideration, for no list of circumstances would ever be really complete. The infinite variety of cases and facets to each case would make general standards either meaning-less "boiler-plate" or a statement of the obvious that no jury would need.

END OF EXAMINATION

FINAL EXAM — CRIMINAL LAW §§ A & B
December 21, 1974

. . . .

THREE PARTS
THREE HOURS
CLOSED BOOK
YOU MAY USE A COPY OF THE U.S. CONSTITUTION
*EACH QUESTION IN SEPARATE BLUE BOOK — AND
YOUR SECTION MUST BE INDICATED*

. . . .

I.

On May 31, 1974, Los Angeles police officer Richard Cron and four other police units conducted a surveillance of the Band Automobile Body Shop which, according to informa-tion obtained by officer Cron from an informant, J. Losh, would be the site of the delivery by one Robert Herdon to Losh of 50 pounds of hashish oil. Cron and his partner were positioned on a nearby rooftop where they had in-stalled a 25 power telescope on a tripod.

The officers observed Herdon arrive at the Body Shop in a Mercedes Benz accompanied by Losh. Almost simul-taneously, a green Pontiac arrived, driven by Clifford Gut-tersund. The three men went to the trunk of the Pontiac, opened it, and Losh then gave a prearranged signal to offi-cer Cron that he had seen the hashish. From Cron's posi-tion, however, he could see nothing in the trunk.

Herdon and Losh then walked away and were out of the

officer's view for 2 to 3 minutes. They returned to Herdon's Mercedes where Losh was shown something in the trunk of that vehicle, whereupon Losh gave another prearranged signal to officer Cron which indicated that the presence of all of the narcotics that were to be delivered had been verified.

At this point several of the officers accosted Herdon and Guttersund, frisking them for weapons. Officer Cron identified himself and asked them if they had any narcotics in their vehicles. Herdon replied in the affirmative but Guttersund replied: "I want to see my lawyer."

While other officers were handcuffing Herdon and Guttersund, Cron searched both vehicles and found a green suitcase in the trunk of the Pontiac and a brown suitcase in the trunk of the Mercedes. The green suitcase was opened by officer Cron at that time and 34 pounds of marijuana was found. The brown suitcase was opened at the police station. It contained 16 additional pounds of marijuana.

What issues would you expect to be raised at the trial of Herdon and Guttersund and how would you expect the court to resolve them?

See People v. Herdon
116 Cal.Rept. 641 (1974)

FINAL EXAM — CRIMINAL LAW §§ A & B
December 21, 1974

. . . .

II.
NEW BLUE BOOK
INDICATE SECTION

After weeks of careful and tedious investigation, the San Francisco police had accumulated considerable evidence that Joseph Stone was involved in a recent rash of robberies and burglaries. Anxious to find his accomplices, as well, they enlisted the aid of a close friend of Stone's, one Jack Brown, who owned the Ajax Bar and Restaurant. Brown was promised "consideration" for his assistance. With Brown's consent, an electronics bug was placed in a bouquet of flowers that served as centerpiece for a corner table in the Ajax Restaurant. Brown then invited Stone to the Restaurant after closing hours where he introduced Stone to William Black, a police under-cover agent posing as a local mobster. During their conversation, Black suggested an elaborate scheme for burglarizing a local department store. Black offered to provide all of the plans and tools for the proposed burglary and suggested that Stone provide three assistants. Stone agreed. This conversation was recorded by the planted bug.

The five men burglarized the department store with considerable ease, but were met at the exit by a phalanx of police who placed them all (except Black, of course) under arrest. Stone shared the back seat of one police vehicle with two of the participants. Unknown to any of them, their conversation was recorded in full by a machine hidden under the floorboards. Incriminating statements were made by all three.

Stone was booked immediately; charged with various felonies; and forced to submit to a fingerprinting and photography session. The fingerprints matched those found at the site of several burglaries.

The following day, Stone was required to participate in a staged line-up where he was identified by several victims of the robberies. That afternoon, two more victims picked out Stone's photograph from a book of "mug shots."

You have been hired as a summer clerk for the lawyer who was appointed to represent Stone. Prepare a memorandum outlining all possible lines of defense strategy and assess the success of each.

FINAL EXAM — CRIMINAL LAW §§ A & B
December 21, 1974

. . . .

III.

NEW BLUE BOOK
INDICATE SECTION

In a recent national telecast, related to a celebrated case where an accused mass-murderer was released by the courts since his trial had been "infected" by admissions made by him without the required Miranda warnings, the following observation was made:

"Either the legal mind alone now understands modern life, or the capacity of everybody else to understand the legal mind has collapsed."

Comment.

END OF EXAM

Final Examination
Constitutional Law (615)   May 28, 1974

Discuss the constitutional issues in each of the following (estimated time for each: 36 minutes):

I.

The American Whiteshirts, a political organization, displays a large sign at the front of its downtown headquarters s⁺ating: Communists, socialists, and Jews are scum and should be exterminated. Those Whiteshirts responsible for putting up the sign are arrested and charged with violation of a state statute prohibiting any publication that insults and degrades a minority group or is likely to provoke violent disorder.

II.

A state statute provides: Every employer shall have the

right to hire or not hire such persons as he chooses. Timid advertises for a retail clerk but, fearing loss of white patronage, refuses to hire Ambitious, a fully-qualified black applicant. Ambitious sues in a state court for an injunction to compel his employment by Timid.

III.

A bill introduced in Congress would impose a 25% tax on the sale of articles manufactured in states that do not require employers to compensate employees and their dependents in full (i.e., without limitation as to amount) for all work-related injuries. (Most workmen's compensation laws limit the amount of the employer's strict liability.)

IV.

A bill introduced in the legislature of the state of Affluence would raise the Affluence minimum wage and forbid the sale in that state of any product produced in a state with a lower minimum wage. (Assume no federal statute.)

V.

Resistant, who is childless, sues in a federal court to enjoin the Secretary of the Treasury from disbursing money, pursuant to a federal statute, to school districts for such expenditures as are approved by the Secretary of Health, Education, and Welfare.

END OF EXAMINATION

USCLC   TORTS
Fall 1974

FINAL EXAMINATION

Question 1 — 1¾ Hours

"The economic news is so gloomy," said Nestucka, "that this just does not seem like the Christmas season." She was seated cross-legged on the couch, facing Paul.

"Why don't we put up some outside Christmas lights this year," asked Paul, "that will brighten your spirits and add color to the neighborhood as well."

"Good idea," she said, "they have taken off those silly regulations banning outside lights, and Christmas lights would indeed make me feel more festive."

Nestucka was mistaken about the regulations. Officials of the City of Plasadena, where they lived, had discussed the possibility of rescinding the ordinances enacted last year banning outdoor lighting "except as necessary for safety purposes." But so far, no official steps had been taken.

Nestucka went the next day to the Hard Ware Co., a retail outlet in Plasadena. There she priced two strings of Christmas lights, both manufactured and distributed by the Brite Light Mfg. Co., a Plasadena concern. Model B210 had twenty lights and cost $16.75; model 260Z had twenty lights and cost $32.50. The B210 model was labeled "Indoor Lights for the Holiday Season;" the 260Z model was labeled "Indoor/Outdoor Holiday Lights." Although Nestucka thought that the 260Z had a somewhat heavier cord connecting the lights to one another, she was unable to see much difference between the two models. Before she purchased, she asked Grimm, a salesperson in the store, whether she could use the model B210 outside. Grimm replied, "sure, if you want to." She then bought the B210.

Nestucka installed the lights herself. When Paul saw the installation, he remarked to himself that the end of the string was rather close to the ground, and he wondered whether the neighborhood kids might not try to "screw around with the lights." But he did not change the installation, and he told Nestucka that the lights looked "swell."

Three days later Plasadena suffered a heavy rainstorm.

Shortly after the rain had stopped, Ms. Brown, a neighbor of Nestucka and Paul, let her pet cat, Richmond, out of her house. Richmond wandered over onto Nestucka's and Paul's property. He climbed onto their roof and began sniffing around the Christmas lights. After chewing the cord a little, he jumped off the roof and started chewing on the light cord precisely at the point where it was closest to the ground. After some chewing, Richmond succeeded in penetrating the insulation and, as his paws were in contact with the damp ground, he was electrocuted, his hair flying straight out and his tail becoming rigid, much like what might be seen in a cartoon.

Just at the moment that Richmond's teeth made contact with the bare wires, Mr. Brown, Ms. Brown's husband, arrived home from a shopping trip to Rears, where he had purchased a shotgun as a present for his mother-in-law. He saw Richmond's plight, and he rushed onto Paul's and Nestucka's property. When he took hold of Richmond, Mr. Brown received a fair jolt from the current being conducted through Richmond's body. Mr. Brown suffered from a heart condition which caused his heart to beat irregularly from time to time and for which he took regular medication. The electric shock caused his heart to beat so irregularly that he lost consciousness, falling on the ground in a heap. Within ten minutes his heart began to fibrilliate, causing his death.

Mr. Smith, another neighbor, had seen Brown go onto Paul's and Nestucka's property, and he observed Brown's collapse. Smith, who had bad eyesight, did not recognize Brown, but he did see that he was carrying a shotgun. Thinking that Brown was a burglar, Smith called the Plasadena police. He unfortunately gave the wrong address to the emergency operator, saying that the trouble was on

Rose *Street* rather than on Rose *Lane*, and due solely to
the incorrect address, the police and the rescue squad did
not arrive until after Brown had expired.

Assume that a wrongful death statute allows Mr. Brown's
estate to sue for injuries to his person or property. Ms.
Brown, administratrix of the estate, consults you for advice. Discuss the potential defendants, the bases of their
liability, and the defenses they might assert.

END OF QUESTION 1

INSTITUTION OF PROPERTY OWNERSHIP
December 1974

I. A owned a house and lot in fee simple. The house was
vacant and the property generally neglected. The swim-
ming pool on the premises was filled with dirt and silt
to a depth of a foot or more. A sold the premises, by
legal description of the real estate, to B and his heirs.
B hired C to clean out the pool. In the process of doing
so, C found a valuable man's diamond ring buried in
the mud. C had the ring cleaned and thereafter wore
it regularly. C became ill and had to undergo major
surgery. As a precaution against theft while the patient was unconscious, the nurse was putting all C's
valuables in an envelope to be held in the hospital safe,
just before C was wheeled into the operating room.
C pulled off the ring, handed it to the nurse, saying,
"Put this ring with the rest. If I don't come through,
I want D to have it." Half way through the surgery,
the surgeon concluded that C had inoperable cancer.
They sewed him up and returned him to his room,
where he died of the cancer a month later. He never

mentioned the ring or other valuables again and they stayed in the safe.

After C's death, the ring was claimed by A, B, D, and C's administrator. Discuss the claim of each.

II. L, who owned Blackacre in fee simple, leased it in writing to T for a term of three years, beginning July 1, 1969, at a rental of $3600 a year, payable in equal monthly installments. T took possession and paid his rent promptly every month. Aside from the rent payments, there was no communication between L and T in 1972. On July 1, 1972, T sent L a check for $300, which L cashed and T continued in possession. On June 15, 1973, T wrote L, "Please take notice that I shall terminate my tenancy of Blackacre and move out on July 14, 1973. Enclosed find my check for $150, being the rent for the first half of July."

L immediately replied, "You have a lease; you can't walk out whenever you please. I return your check and I shall expect $300 on the first of each month for the next two years."

On July 14, T moved out and sent L the keys and (again) the check for $150. L wrote, "I do not accept your surrender of the premises. I accept the check only as payment on account. I shall endeavor to re-let the premises on your account and hold you responsible for any loss." T replied, "I have quit the premises and owe you nothing. You are on your own."

On September 1, 1973, L let the premises to X until

June 30, 1974, at a rent of $200 a month. X paid promptly and moved out June 30, 1974, since when the premises have been vacant.

On August 1, 1974, L brought an action vs. T for $1750, computed as $300 rent for July, 1973; $300 rent for August, 1973; $300 rent for July, 1974; $1000 differential September 1973–June 1974, less $150 on account.

What theory or theories support L's claims? What defenses has T?

III. A successful novel recorded the will of one of its principal characters, a wealthy and elderly bachelor, in substantially these terms. "I devise and bequeath all my estate, real and personal, to my nephew, Soames, to be held by him and his successors upon trust. He is to invest the same, and all income received during the duration of the trust shall be added to the principal and re-invested. The trust shall terminate 21 years after the death of the last survivor of the linial descendants of my grandfather, Jolyan, living at my death, at which time the principal and accumulated income shall be distributed absolutely to the linial descendants of my grandfather, Jolyan, then living, the share of each of such descendants to be determined by right of representation."

Does this passage suggest that novelists should get legal opinion before they write on legal subjects? Why or why not?

IV. To the delight of the legal profession, Testator pre-

pared and executed his own will. He owned Goldenacre
in fee simple and his will read, "I leave my beloved
Goldenacre to my two sisters, Hilda and Hepzibah. I
want them to live together on Goldenacre and never to
sell it. If either of my said sisters dies, the other shall
have and enjoy all of Goldenacre absolutely."

Several years after Testator's death, the relations between Hilda and Hepzibah became strained. For valuable consideration, Hepzibah executed a deed purport-
ing to convey all her right, title, and interest in Goldenacre to Hazel. Not long thereafter, Hepzibah died. Who
is entitled to how much of Goldenacre and why?

CONTRACTS   December 1974
Question No. 1
Jim Forman worked for years putting together a real
estate transaction by which he obtained a 35-year lease
on some beachfront property in Northern California for a
resort and a boys' and girls' summer camp. Unfortunately,
just a few weeks after he had signed all the papers to obtain the leasehold, but before he had begun construction
of the buildings and facilities he needed, the State Legislature enacted the Coastal Environment Protection Act, which
required all new beachfront construction to be licensed. He
quickly learned, however, that the act contained a "grandfather clause" entitling anyone who had obtained his property interest before the act's enactment and who had "in
good faith" already adopted a planned course of construction, to obtain a construction license. Jim applied for a construction license under the "grandfather clause."
The state official who was assigned to investigate Jim's
case was Bill Baker. The investigation began in the spring.
Had all gone smoothly, a license would have been obtained

in one or two weeks, in plenty of time for Jim to begin and complete construction that year, before the weather turned bad in the fall, so as to be in operation the year after. But Baker deliberately delayed until Jim was desperate and then told Jim that he would be able to get him his license if, and only if, Jim would promise to employ him as the resort's publicity director. Fearing that if he had to wait the extra year his money would run out, Jim agreed. Jim said the position would pay $25,000 per year and would be open for Bill as soon as construction was completed. In the course of these negotiations Jim asked what assurance he had that Bill's quick employment in the project as soon as he quit his state job would not be noticed, so that both of them would get into legal trouble. Bill replied that no one ever followed up on what jobs a state employee took after he quit.

The license was issued, construction was completed in October, Bill quit his state job and entered Jim's employment in November. The two men signed an employment contract reciting that Bill was hiring Jim only because he was very impressed with his abilities as a state official and that the hiring had nothing whatever to do with Bill's role in getting Jim's license. The contract provided further that Bill was to be paid $25,000 per year, for three years' minimum, and that Bill could be fired "only for willful neglect of his duties."

Unknown to Bill, the state has a policy of following up on the jobs which its employees in sensitive positions take after they leave state employment. Bill's position with the state was considered sensitive. Jim's lawyer informed Jim of this fact after Jim confessed to him, just this month (December), what had happened. Jim immediately fired Baker. Although Baker had worked only a few weeks, Jim already felt that he would not be a good publicity director, but Baker had not wilfully neglected any of his duties.

You are the judge and the case is yours to decide without a jury. Forman's lawyer has pleaded mistake and lack of consideration. Baker's lawyer has pleaded the parol evidence rule as a bar to the admission of evidence of the parties' alleged prior oral agreement. You have found as a fact that everything happened just as above stated. In addition, it now appears quite certain that the state has no intested in following up on Baker's case for the purpose of bringing criminal action. The state prosecutor says that there are several technicalities in the law which would almost certainly prevent his getting a conviction against Baker in a conflict-of-interest prosecution; technically, he says, Baker did nothing which constitutes a violation.

Decide the case and give your reasons. Rule on each of the specific issues the parties have raised and, in addition, on any others which you believe are pertinent.

Question No. 2

Green is a manufacturer of toy cars. White is a rubber goods manufacturer. In the spring, in anticipation of building up a large inventory of toys for the Christmas trade by manufacturing during the fall and summer, Green signed agreements with various suppliers of parts and materials. White is one of several firms with which Green signed agreements for supplying the toy tires to go on its toy trucks. The agreement between Green and White reads:

"CONTRACT

"Between the instant date, which is April 3, 1974, and December 1, 1974, White will sell and Green will buy the toy tires which meet the specifications set forth below at a price of \$75 per thousand. Delivery will be within 10 working days of the receipt by White of Green's orders.

Provided that Green will never without White's consent order more than 50,000 tires per month.

"(. . . the specifications for the tires . . .)

"This contract cannot be changed or amended in any way except by a writing signed by both of the parties hereto."

(signed)

Green

(signed)

White

White delivered thousands of tires to Green pursuant to the agreement until August 1st, when there was a sudden, substantial rise in the price of rubber on the international rubber market. White telephoned Green and explained what had happened and asked for a price increase to $95 per thousand. Green agreed. The parties confirmed their agreement by letters sent to each other the same day. Several thousand tires were sold during the next two weeks at the new price.

On August 15th White still had 50,000 tires to make on orders which Green had given to him during the preceding week. On that day he received from Green in the mail an order for another 50,000. After receiving the order he received a telephone call from Green, who had been reading in the newspapers about new disturbances in the international rubber market and was worried. Green told White that he, Green, had to commit his toy trucks to large department store chains in advance, at set prices, and that he therefore needed White's assurance that "all the 50,000 tires I have just ordered" will be delivered at $95 per thousand "regardless of what happens to the rubber price." Thinking that Green was referring to the 50,000 tires which had been ordered the week before but still not delivered,

White replied, "Sure, no problem." White thought there was no problem as to the tires previously ordered because he had already purchased the rubber for them.

The price of rubber did advance substantially after their telephone call. White then telephoned Green to ask for a price increase above $95 for tires on the most recent order. Green refused, reminding White of the previous telephone call. White then learned to his dismay that he had inadvertently agreed to freeze the price on the new order, not on the tires as yet undelivered on the previous orders, so he told Green of his mistake and said, "I'm sorry, I cannot hold the price at less than $110." Green refused to go up a cent, so White said, "Then I cancel the whole contract!" Green answered, "You can't. It says right in the contract that you can't do anything to it unless we both consent in writing, and I won't consent. I've already signed contracts with six department store chains for toy trucks which I will lose money on if you advance your price."

The two men finally agreed that White would deliver all the tires that Green had ordered and that they would let a judge decide whether or not White was entitled to charge a higher price. They also agreed that if White was entitled to charge more, he would charge $110 a thousand. You are the judge. Give your reasons and decide the case.

CONTRACTS   May 1974
Question No. 1
(1½ hour) (Word limit: 1000)

Tom Baxter was a star football player at his university. Prior to his graduation this year, he signed a three-year contract with the Yakima Goats, a professional football team, for a bonus of $25,000. The contract obligates the Goats to employ him, and him to play for the Goats, for three years for an annual salary of $35,000 (in addition to the bonus). The contract provides that the salary is to continue for the full three years despite any injuries Tom may receive while playing which disable him and, on the other hand, that Tom shall not engage in certain dangerous sports, such as skiing, climbing, etc., either during or between seasons for the life of the contract.

Tom graduated May 1st and proceeded at once to spring training. In the opinion of the Goats coach, he did not perform well. After only two weeks of training, on May 15th, he was dropped from the team along with some other rookie players. All the dropped players were given one month's salary and the price of an airline ticket home. None of the other dropped players had contracts.

As soon as he got home Tom got a lawyer and brought suit against the Goats for breach of contract, demanding that he be taken back as a player for the promised three-year period. The case was set for early hearing because of the circumstances and the nature of the relief demanded. You are the judge.

When Tom comes into court he is on crutches. His lawyer tells you that he was hit by a car yesterday, while walking across the street on his way to a movie, and that the accident was entirely the driver's fault. The accident will disable Tom from playing football for three years. Decide the case and give your reasons. The rules of civil procedure of your court (as is true of most courts today) allow a judge to grant whatever relief would be appropriate, regardless of the relief originally requested.

Question No. 2
(2½ hours) (Word limit: 1800)

Truck Corporation manufactures trucks. Steel Corporation manufactures steel. Truck Corporation contracted with Steel Corporation for the purchase of 52,000 tons of steel for the following year. The steel was to be delivered in 52 equal installments of 1000 tons no later than Tuesday of each week, payable cash on delivery at the rate of $175 per ton plus delivery charges. Delivery was to be to whichever of Truck's five plants Truck designated, and shipping instructions were to be given by Truck to Steel no later than the Wednesday preceding each week. The steel was to be "Grade Triple A," which is a grade known throughout the steel and automotive industries as being fit for the construction of truck and automobile engines. All Truck's plants are within 300 miles of Steel's plant, and all are on connecting railroad lines.

The time for commencement of deliveries came and went, and the contract was performed without a hitch for ten weeks, with one exception. Three of the deliveries consisted of steel which was not quite Grade Triple A. Truck accepted the shipments anyway, because the insufficiency was slight and the steel was, in fact, sufficiently good to be usable in Truck's engines.

Then, an economic upturn in Western Europe made steel there in short supply, European steel manufacturers cut down on their exports in order to meet their increased domestic demand, so steel also became in short supply in the United States. Car Corporation is a manufacturer of automobiles. Unlike Truck Corporation, Car Corporation had no long-term supply contract with a steel manufacturer. It preferred to take its chances on the open market. The sudden domestic shortage caught it short. Truck, on the other hand, realized that it had, and probably would continue to have, more steel than it would need, because truck sales had dropped substantially because of the energy crisis.

Truck and Car reached an agreement whereby, in exchange for a payment by Car to Truck of $400,000 cash, Car could take 250 tons out of the 1000 tons which Truck received from Steel every week. Car would, in addition, pay Steel $175 per ton plus delivery charges. All Car's plants were within the same general area as were Truck's, all were on railroad lines connecting with the same railroad systems, and all were within 300 miles of Steel's plant. The parties signed their agreement, and Car delivered to Truck a $400,000 check.

The next Wednesday, Truck Corporation telephoned Steel Corporation with delivery instructions for 750 tons. Car Corporation telephoned Steel delivery instructions for 250 tons and, at the same time, informed Steel of its agreement with Truck. Steel made both shipments. Then, suddenly, because of the domestic shortage, the Federal Government ordered large steel users not to buy steel unless they first obtained a government permit. The permits were to be issued on the basis of proven need. Car Corporation had no trouble getting a permit to cover all its purchases, but Truck Corporation was unable to justify a need for more than 750 tons. The Government also ordered steel manufacturers not to make any large shipments (anything over 50 tons) without first obtaining a copy of the purchaser's permit.

The next week Truck and Car both telephoned their shipping instructions to Steel and also mailed to Steel copies of their permits. Steel made the shipments in time, but the steel this time was not quite Grade Triple A. Truck accepted its shipment anyway, but Car rejected the shipment to it. Steel was able to re-sell the rejected shipment at a profit, because of the shortage, but Car, also because of the shortage, was unable to find good enough steel to construct its engines elsewhere and, after two days, had to shut down some of its assembly lines. The line shutdowns cost it $50,000 per day in standby maintenance costs and union layoff benefits. In the ensuing arguments between officers of Car and officers of Steel, the Steel officers refused to give any assurances that all future shipments would be Grade Triple A. They said that their manufacturing process was not capable of making such quality steel every time, without variation. Since the officers of Car were unwilling to say that they would accept any shipments which were not Triple A, Steel informed both Car and Truck that it considered the contract terminated.

Because of bank-clearance delays, the $400,000 check has not yet cleared Car's account. Car stopped payment on it. Car also sues both Truck and Steel. Its complaint against Steel asks for both damages and specific performance. Truck sues Car on the check. Steel sues Truck for whatever damages it may be liable to Car, although it maintains that it is not liable for any. The contract between Truck and Steel contains a clause which reads, "This contract is not assignable by either party without the prior written consent of the other."

The cases have been consolidated for trial in your court. Decide them and give your reasons.

Notes